ENDORS[T0247378

This is simply genius. A practical, easy-to-read guide to getting coverage for your small business.

Bex Burn-Callander, former enterprise editor, *The Telegraph*

PR has a deservedly bad reputation, which is why this book is so important, Lucy's ideas for what PR is, and what it's not, serve as a blueprint for what it should, and could be. Essential bullshit-free guidance in a bullshit-rich industry. I wish we'd had this book when we were starting out, in fact I wish the PR industry had read this book when it was starting out.

Sam Conniff, Author of *Be More Pirate*, Founder of Livity

In an industry rife with jargon and snake oil, Lucy demystifies the dark arts of PR and cuts to the chase showing founders everywhere how to get the word out faster, more authentically and without a massive price tag. An essential read for anyone who wants to build a strong profile for their business or themselves.

Jeff Tayler, Editor in Chief, Courier Media

Every small business should take its reputation seriously, and *Hype Yourself* is a fantastic hands-on guide for business managers up and down the country. If you're looking for a practical book to help you manage your own PR, look no further.

Francis Ingham, Director General, PRCA

What makes this book so special is Lucy's clear focus and passion for delivering actionable content to small businesses. In a world where we are inundated with digital marketing campaigns, curating a more genuine connection with potential/actual customers is ever more important. This book is a beautifully written insight into how anyone can start building themselves a strong PR campaign that works for their business.

Albert Azis-Clauson, CEO & Founder of UnderPinned

Covering so much more than just PR, *Hype Yourself* is a must-read for any business owner wanting to build awareness in an authentic and genuine way. This book cuts the fluff and gives you straight talking PR advice that you can action before you plough any more time or money into PR. Lucy's thinking is outside the traditional PR box: refreshing and inspiring.

Rosie Davies-Smith, Founder of PR Dispatch & LFA

I've always admired Lucy and her approach towards her clients, she really knows her stuff – and this book is proof of that. Having worked in the PR industry for nearly 15 years, it's very refreshing to see professionals in our industry offering solutions that aren't just based on the highest price point. To someone with no knowledge of the PR world, it can seem intimidating and difficult to get started – however this book breaks that barrier down and makes it a world that everyone can be a part of. I would recommend this book to anyone starting their own business, it gives a clear, step by step guide to creating a full PR plan.

Nicky Marks, Managing Director, Census Wide

I loved this book as it is basically everything you need to know in order to avoid paying huge fees to PR agencies. It takes a really modern can-do approach, demystifies the whole process of publicising yourself or your project and walks you through how to do it step by step. Lucy has a snappy, straight-to-the-point way of writing and avoids all the usual PR clichés which is a relief. Mercifully it is also waffle-free. When I speak at events about my business life I often get asked if I can recommend PR services – which I have always been reluctant to as it's such a hard thing to measure and so expensive – now I can just say READ THIS INSTEAD.

Fleur Emery, Startup expert and columnist at *Courier Magazine*

I first saw Lucy speak at a marketing event and was blown away with the valuable tips, tricks and hacks in the presentation – so I was ready to scratch and kick to make sure I was first in line to get 200+ pages more of Lucy's great PR insights! *Hype yourself* more than lives up to the hype – the format makes it easy to understand and provides context to see how it can be implemented with great real world examples. I have been working through and preparing my PR toolkit and signposting our bootstrapping businesses to do the same! I'm a full on believer of the hype and can't wait to hype myself!

Simon Magness, Enterprise Education Projects Officer,
Cass Business School

No waffle. No fluff. This book is chock-a-block with punchy, practical PR advice that will have you buzzing with ideas right from the start. Every small business needs good PR. Every small business owner needs to read this book.

Frankie Tortora, *Doing It For The Kids*

It's official, I'm calling it 'The Subtle Art of Being Your Own Cheerleader!' Save your money on PR stunts. This masterpiece is all you need to be your own Boss.

John Furno, General Assembly London

HYPE YOURSELF

A NO-NONSENSE PR TOOLKIT FOR SMALL BUSINESSES

LUCY WERNER

First published in Great Britain by Practical Inspiration Publishing, 2020

© Lucy Werner, 2020

The moral rights of the author have been asserted

ISBN   978-1-78860-123-8 (print)
       978-1-78860-122-1 (epub)
       978-1-78860-121-4 (mobi)

Practical Inspiration
PUBLISHING

TABLE OF CONTENTS

DEDICATION

For my sunshine Hadrien, who always hypes me and
helps me to keep on hyping everyone else.

FOREWORD

Jim Cregan, co-founder of Jimmy's Iced Coffee

When we launched Jimmy's Iced Coffee, we had large production runs of product with a relatively short shelf life, which meant we had to do everything in our power to get the word out to as many people as possible, as quickly as possible.

And that meant becoming the ultimate company prostitute. We sold ourselves wherever we went. We would pull people over in the street to try our product, interrupt surfers returning from the waves, accountants legging it onto the tube and more, way way more.

What I love most about PR is the actual meaning of the phrase: Public Relations. The relationship we have with the public and how we want to behave around them. It's worth thinking about that. PR is so much more than just a black book and a hefty bill at The Ivy in return for a feature in a trade mag.

Lucy really understood what we were and what we stood for, making it an honest joy to work with her, and she generated some awesome 'hype' for us. If you can't have her working with you in person, this book is the next best thing – read it, then get out there and hype yourself!

INTRODUCTION

Welcome to *Hype Yourself.* My name is Lucy and I have over 15 years' experience in communications, working both inhouse and for some of London's top PR agencies. These days, I run a communications consultancy and training hub at www.thewern.com, for small businesses and entrepreneurs. I handle the PR and my partner does design and branding, so we are a one-stop shop to launch and grow new or independent companies.

I was sick of working for brands that had no heart and wanted to work with businesses that I cared about and people I liked to give them affordable PR solutions. In the last five years, I've personally worked with over 100 entrepreneurs globally, but there are millions of founders who can't afford basic PR costs or even realise the value, which is why I wanted to write this book.

Publicity takes time and research but with consistency (and other than the cost of your time), you can transform your business for free. Unlike other PR book authors, I'm walking my own talk, continually learning and evolving my own craft so that I can pass this knowledge on to you. I've seen first-hand how transformative promoting myself has been for my own business as well as that of my clients.

Hyping myself landed me a book deal, national newspaper coverage, paid-for speaking gigs, teaching opportunities, invitations to appear on podcasts and allowed me to increase my consultancy fees.

But don't just take my word for it, have a read through of the multiple expert tips, client examples and journalist hacks that I've collated to give you as many tangible takeaways as possible to promote your business.

What is PR?

PR is more than just telling your story to journalists. It is anything you do that is in the public eye and, I believe, is the best free tool that should be part of your marketing mix. Unlike advertising, where you are visible for as long as you pay to be, publicity has no shelf life.

Any time you are responding in the public eye, you have an opportunity to hype yourself. This might look like:

- Talking to new connections at an event
- How you respond in a crisis
- What you post on Instagram
- How you launch a product
- The tactics you use to drive email sign-ups
- Your mechanics to encourage positive mentions and awareness around your business
- Your company blog
- An industry report or whitepaper
- Speaking engagements.

And a great publicist will work with you to help you strategically steer all of this as well as generate creative campaigns to get your message out there. They may even push back on what you think you know about your business, and believe me, that is OK because sometimes what we think is the most interesting thing about our business is not what others think.

What PR is not

One of the biggest mistakes I see is people thinking that PR is writing a press release and issuing it to a contacts list, what is known in the industry as 'spray and pray'. This is absolutely the worst thing that any PR practitioner or business owner could do; whilst we are clearing up myths, PR is not:

- An opportunity for you to tell a journalist what to write – e.g., a whole one-page feature on your business saying how great/different/new/unique it is
- A paid-for promotional or marketing piece of copy (this is an advert)
- All about the contacts in your address book (obviously, this helps, but some of the best pieces of coverage I have secured were through bespoke and tailored emails and doing my research)
- An excuse to take a journalist out for a long lunch and get them drunk enough to write about you (we are not living in a Wolf of Wall Street era, my friends).

And the grey area in between

- Social media/influencer engagement is argued by some to be part of the PR mix, some people see it as a specialist skill and others think it is the job of digital marketing agencies. Whatever your view, it needs to be part of your PR toolkit so we will spend some time learning the ropes on this.
- Search engine optimisation (SEO)/website design/ branding – again there are specialist agencies that focus on each of these elements and some PR agencies also offer this service. And again, what I will say is that if you have not considered these, then with the best PR in your world you will struggle to get as much traction. If someone can't understand what you are about just from your branding and website, then consider investing in this before hyping yourself.

Why do I need a self-hype book?

It is totally commonplace to spend time on self-love, but your business doesn't need a self-help book; if your budgets are tight and you need help with sales, awareness, opportunities, connections or are struggling to put your face at the front of your work, then you need some self-hype.

Put simply, people buy people. The *Hype Yourself* mission is to make sure that you are doing everything you can to showcase who you are, so that you can build that emotional connection with your audience.

We are inundated by branding, advertising and companies pushing us to purchase. If Brexit or Donald Trump taught us anything, it's that consumers make decisions based on emotions not statistics.

Consumers engage with the people behind brands because it helps them understand how the brand fits with their own identity. When you share who you are and what you are about you don't even need to sell to your audience anymore because they have bought into you.

We are seeing even larger companies shifting towards this trend, but entrepreneurs are lucky in that they have the agility and personality to become their own content creators easily.

I want you to be one of the first people to take advantage of this shifting trend.

If you can learn to treat yourself with as much time and respect as one of your own clients and you follow just some of the suggestions in this book, you will have a free tap that you can turn on at any point for new opportunities, and unlike advertising or marketing, this can be executed at no cost to your business.

I'm not just a huge fan of publicity because I work in it – I'm a living case study of someone who PRs herself every day. I have successfully built a six-figure lifestyle business based entirely on using the art to Hype Myself. Below are just some of the ways that publicity could help you:

- When you Google your business/name, what comes up? If you are not easily searchable it can affect your sales as people can't find you. But an effective PR campaign will drive up your search engine optimisation (SEO) and make you more visible without having to spend on Google AdWords.
- One of the most expensive costs to any business is acquiring new customers. Publicity can help you reach a larger audience in a more authentic and engaging way and it doesn't disappear when the budget runs out. Your media mentions will live online.
- With millions of businesses out there you need to keep front of mind; the successful businesses we remember have founders who understand (or understood) the importance of publicity – think Richard Branson, Steve Jobs, Brené Brown.
- PR-ing yourself means you are forced to constantly evolve, which is the foundation of all business success. By staying on the metaphorical shop floor and creating new content to promote your business, you keep yourself informed and your ideas fresh.
- We are in an era of whoever shouts the loudest wins, whether that is shouting about your brilliant work or your innovative thinking. If you are not part of the conversation, then no one will see what you are doing.

- It is cheaper to retain customers than to find new ones; hyping yourself will arm you with resources to keep your current audience engaged and receptive, assisting with repeat business.

OK, so how is *this* book specifically going to help me with my PR?

I'm going to hand-hold you through the same PR process I use for myself and my clients. I start off every PR talk I do with a picture of my Dad, Fred – because he was the person who taught me to always prepare before doing a job. I always think of PR as like a marathon, because it takes practice, showing up and consistency. If you were a running novice, you'd be seeking advice on which running shoes to buy (or at least I hope you would) and following a training programme. Yes, you can just put shoes on and run and for some people this works out alright. But to avoid injury, insult and to be the absolute best you can be, you put the work in which is what this book will help you do for self-hype.

Each chapter works as a functional toolkit. I recommend using the book chronologically but the format does allow you to dip in and out of relevant sections when needed. Every element is split into:

- Activity: step-by-step instructions to activate this for your own business

- Example: a client, industry or self-example of what this might look like in action
- Tips: expert or best-in-practice tips to ensure that you execute to the best of your abilities
- Checklist: a review of what we have just covered
- Chapter summary: at the end of each chapter I'll cover what you should have ticked off and what is coming up next.

Each chapter follows a clear road map to build your press office.

Chapter 1: PR plan – this is where we put the co-ordinates in your GPS, so we know where we are ending up on our publicity journey. Otherwise, we are going to be blindly waving our arms around in the PR pool not knowing which direction we are heading in. This chapter will provide clarity to shape your programme.

Chapter 2: Master your media toolkit – before you even think about contacting a journalist or pitching yourself as an expert for a podcast you need to get your house in order. This chapter is going to get into the practical minutiae of everything you need in your PR artillery before we go into our hype battle.

Chapter 3: Starting your press office – this is where I will hand over all the gems I've discovered for finding your way around the publicity wilderness. It can be a jungle out there and even for a seasoned PR professional you might only hear crickets. So, this section is a practical step-by-step list of actions to get you out there.

Chapter 4: The brain farts – this chapter aims to help ignite your creative thinking for your press office. It's not all about big budgets but if you do have a bit of money in the pot or want some help generating quick creative wins, then this chapter will help you think far beyond the press release.

By the end of this book I want you to be well on your way to running a successful PR campaign, with well-thought-through building blocks. And the best bit, unlike any other publicity officer, *you* are already an expert in your business. So, who is better to talk about it?

OK. Grab your notebook if you haven't already and let's get hyping.

WHAT YOU WILL NEED

- A notebook to complete all of the tasks or download the relevant PDFs from www.thewern.com/book to fill in as you go along
- A red pen, time to be your own school teacher
- A 12-month wall chart to mark your key PR events

xx | Hype Yourself

- A good relationship with your local newsagent so that you can call in niche magazines when needed – it is advisable to have an account so you can buy magazines in bulk.

CHAPTER 1

PR PLAN

OK, I'm going to start by throwing you into the deep end, ahead of strategic thinking. For this chapter, I want you to have an organised declutter hat on. Imagine your current PR strategy is a pile of dirty laundry and this is the Marie Kondo process to have some neat clothes at the end.

By the end of this chapter you will have laid the foundations for an effective campaign. It is an essential road map for your self-hype journey and makes you think into the why and what of your business – I'll ask you regularly to refer to this throughout the book.

I am amazed at how many people (including PRs) are carrying out campaigns with no overarching strategy. Success can already be hard enough to measure without setting some goals and there is no point putting all the hard work in to hype yourself if you don't know why you are doing it. We will now run through the following:

- – Business objectives
- – Communications objectives

- – Your why
- – Audience
- – What is unique about your business
- – Communications calendar
- – Crisis Q&A.

Grab your notebook or download the strategy template from www.thewern.com/book. Throughout the book I will provide various business examples, but for the strategy work in Chapter 1 I have used my own business as a case study. The full template for this is also available from the website.

1.1 Business objectives

We need to start with outlining your business objectives, which we will constantly remind ourselves of all the way through. It is nigh on impossible to hype yourself in an effective way without knowing these, so best to get them sorted from the beginning. Changing the goals halfway through the campaign means you may have to start from scratch, so it is essential that your business targets are outlined on one page.

ACTIVITY

In your workbook write down the title 'Business objectives', have a read through the following questions and answer the questions that feel relevant for your own business.

NB: You don't have to have an answer for all of these pillars, I've just included some examples to get you thinking.

Turnover or business growth

- Do you want to get more bums on seats?
- Do you want to launch or sell more products?
- What are your revenue goals?
- How much website traffic are you looking to attract?
- How many email sign-ups are you looking for?
- What's your social media following target?

Internal goals

- Are you looking to find brilliant industry talent to come work with you?
- Do you want to empower existing employees to be industry experts?
- Which areas of your business do you need training or assistance with?

Operational

- Can you improve on any element of your supply chain to improve profitability?
- Are all logistical elements of your business up to scratch?

Industry/customer awareness

- Are you looking to secure alternative revenue streams where you need to raise your own industry profile?
- Do you want to be considered as a major player within your niche?
- Do you need to reach a wider audience?
- Do you need to boost awareness within a specific demographic?

EXAMPLE

At the beginning of 2019, this is what business objectives looked like for The Wern.

Revenue

- Increase revenue streams from consultancy to coaching, books, teaching, courses and products.
- Increase turnover by 50%.

Operational

- Review effectiveness of current suppliers and contracts.

Growth

- Establish email marketing database.
- Grow existing social media channels by 200%.

Awareness

- Grow my profile as a PR expert for small businesses and entrepreneurs to underpin the above goals.

TIPS

- Your business objectives should be brief and to the point.
- A business goal shouldn't read like an essay, make it achievable.
- A measurable goal means that everyone who is working on the business is heading for the same direction.
- Double-check that your business objectives also fit your personal objectives.

1.2 Communications objectives

The next header in the template or your own workbook is for your communications objectives. For this segment, I want you to think about how and why you want to hype yourself. From your business objectives we have an end goal, but this activity is to dig deeper into the voice you will use to hype yourself. The best relationships are based on truth and in order to hype your business we need to help pull out the voice of the true you.

ACTIVITY

Think about the following questions:

- Are you trying to establish yourself as a voice of authority? In what area?
- Are you an entertainer?
- Do you want to be a quirky, fun brand? Or are you trying to educate consumers about a new product category?
- Is there an education role in explaining your business offering?
- What is unique to your business personality?
- Can you describe your tone of voice?
- Can you use adjectives that mimic your true personality?

EXAMPLE

To accompany The Wern's business objectives, I started the year off with the following communications objectives:

- A no-nonsense industry expert that is friendly but direct
- Keeping honest by sharing business vulnerabilities and lessons learnt on the journey
- To lead by example, demonstrate how I use PR to amplify my own business.

TIPS

- Take some time to really think about communications objectives.
- Check against your business goals.
- If there are multiple staff in your business, consider different objectives for each member.
- This is about how you speak.

1.3 Your why

Before we proceed, I want you to stop and check. What is motivating you? Why are these your business goals and how have you come to the decision that you want to communicate in this way?

ACTIVITY

In your notebook under the header 'Why' consider the following questions to determine your motivation.

- Where are you now with your business?
- Is this a side-hustle or do you want it to be your full-time business?
- Do you want to travel for work and does this business allow that?
- Are you hoping to grow a team?
- Do you want to secure investment?
- Would you like to one day sell your company?
- Is this a lifestyle business?

- Do you want your business to fit around childcare/family responsibilities?
- Think deeply about why you want to grow.
- Where do you want to be?

EXAMPLE

These are the whys behind my business, each step digs a little deeper:

- The current PR agency model doesn't work for most of the emerging SME market in the UK. I want to provide an à la carte menu of services to cater for different needs.
- I love PR and want to share my knowledge to help other business owners learn how to promote their own services.
- I care about independent businesses that care about people and I don't want them wasting money on PR agencies if they can do it for themselves.
- A work/life balance is important to me and this is a trait that is also prevalent in many independent businesses.
- I want to build a business where I spend less time being busy and more time on delivering publicity advice that has big impact for individuals.
- Having enough time and money was always an issue in my house as a child. I want to build a business that means I have the time to look after myself and my family.

TIPS

- Don't be afraid to keep looking at the personal reasons underneath your business why.
- There is the good reason why you run your business and then there is the real reason; knowing what motivates your business will focus how you hype it.
- Your audience will care more about what *you* are about and what drives you than what your business does, this must underpin everything that you do.

CHECKLIST

- Are you constantly referring back to your why – before executing any new element of your promotional campaign?
- Are you being honest with yourself about your real motivations as to what drives you to do what you do?

1.4 Audience

Back to the maps, who are you helping and what is their need? For this section, I want you to determine exactly who your ideal customer is, because once we know this, we can then look into how to reach them. You might also benefit from a service offering that is tailored to different customers at different points in their business journeys which is fine. Just make sure you map out for each of them.

ACTIVITY

Try creating an imaginary persona for your ideal client. It can be brilliant to have this person at front of mind as a reminder every time you execute part of your press office.

In your notebook, work through the following questions under two headings 'Audience' and 'Media':

Audience: Who is your target audience?

What is their name, how old are they? Where do they live? Who do they live with? What are their hobbies?

Can you sketch them or cut out a picture from a magazine to help you visualise?

Media: Where are your audience?

Do they watch YouTube? Are they reading magazines? Where do they get their news from? What influences their purchasing decisions? What are their preferred social media channels? Do they read traditional print media, or do they prefer broadcast?

What you need by the end of this task are two lists. Your specific target audience and the different target media they consume.

EXAMPLE

I'm currently focused on a zero to Forbes client – by that I mean someone who has no press exposure and wants to build their profile to a certain level. I'm not interested in the Forbes to TED Talk-type customer (currently); therefore, my business objectives and target audience are skewed to a very specific early-stage customer.

Below is a summary of my two different audiences.

1. *Target Group 1*: Start-up business/entrepreneurs – based in London, in shared workspaces, attending a lot of panel events. Age between 20 and 60, equal male/female split.

   Media: Startups.co.uk, *Courier Magazine*, Telegraph Connect, *Wired*, *Forbes*, *Jolt*, Monocle Entrepreneurs, Secret Leaders.

2. *Target Group 2*: Creative freelancers, side-hustlers, e.g., sole traders or creative networking groups, Mum's the Word Events, Mothers Meeting, No Bull School, UnderPinned, Federation of Small Businesses.

   Media: Women's lifestyle, e.g., *Stylist*, *Marie Claire*, *Cosmopolitan*, Women Who ParentsinBiz, DIFTK (Doing it for the Kids).

TIPS

- If you have a few audience segments, then make sure you do this exercise in depth for them all.
- The more specific you can be, the easier it is to reach them; people are often scared to niche their targeting, but this is proven to be the most effective.
- If you aren't sure what media they consume or want to get a better idea – then just ask them! Do a simple research exercise on surveymonkey. com, perhaps offering an incentive to drive participants to help you.
- Don't let your ego get distracted by your competitive set; being in an industry publication might win you points amongst your peers, but does it move the needle with your target audience?

1.5 What is unique about your business?

What instantly makes every business different is the individuals that are behind it. For this task, I want you to reinforce the foundations of Hype Yourself by doing some clearer thinking on what makes you and your business different. There is no such thing as a new idea but every person has their own thumbprint.

ACTIVITY

To help you think about your unique selling point (USP) you need to identify what separates you from other businesses, so you don't get lost in the crowd.

Under the heading 'USP' in your workbook, do the following exercise:

- List all the benefits and features of your business.
- Put an asterisk against any of the things on this list that only you can say (and not your competitors).
- What is your signature style? Are you extremely strategic, funny, creative, practical, understated? List the words that describe your approach.
- Using all of the above, create sentences that are short, clear and concise and easily understandable.
- Cross-reference against your competitor. If they can be applied, go back to the drawing board.

EXAMPLE

- The Wern is founded by Lucy Werner, an anti-PR for startups and entrepreneurs.

TIPS

- Keep out jargon – make it easy for anyone to understand.
- Can you demonstrate how you address a need?

- Test and refine with your customers if need be – ask 5–10 people for feedback.
- Take your USP and apply it to your competitors, can they say the same? If it can work for any other business, then go back to the drawing board and make sure it is unique for you.

1.6 Communications calendar

Marketeers or social media strategists often refer to this as your content calendar. Planning out your key moments, framing your year and referring to this regularly are crucial tactics in reminding you how and when to hype yourself. A post on the LinkedIn marketing solutions blog states that marketeers with a plan are 60% more likely to be effective with their content marketing than those without.[1] So, don't skip this part.

ACTIVITY

Either download our calendar template for A3 (from www.thewern.com/book) or sketch out a 12-month table – see the example below for a suggestion – and work through the following titles under each month.

---

[1] https://business.linkedin.com/marketing-solutions/blog/content-marketing-webcasts/2016/6-reasons-why-you-should-create-a-content-calendar

Business dates

- What are the key moments in your business for the year ahead?
- Do you have a business birthday?
- Do you have a significant planned new senior hire?
- Do you have an annual charity day?
- Are you implementing an innovative HR policy that you could promote?
- Do you have case studies to promote?
- Are you launching a new product or service?

Key calendar days

Have a Google of national days that relate to your sector; e.g., if you are a food & drink business, Google 'national days for food & drink' and see what comes up that could be applicable to your business:

- If you are a business-to-business (B2B) organisation, there are still plenty of national days that can be applicable. What about National Coworking Day, National Work from Home Day, National Apprenticeship Week, Small Business Saturday or National Freelancers Day as a starter for 10?
- What about key moments such as the budget, or policy debate days that might apply to your business? Check what is coming up in parliament for inspiration.

- Each month we share our own cultural calendar
  dates via our blog and Instagram on @wernchat;
  have a look out for inspiration on dates relating
  to sport, fashion, film, design and TV.

Think about how you can do something different on
a traditional newshook. Grace Gould from Soda Says
shows just how innovative you can be:

> Our favourite case of using a calendar newshook
> to our advantage was when Soda Says launched
> our Sex Tech edit for Valentines Day 2019. We
> did a whole series of programming around
> demystifying female pleasure and self love. We
> even co-hosted a sold out "unValentines Day"
> party with the Pink Protest and the Libreria
> bookstore in East London.

Awards/conferences/panels

- Think about how you could populate your
  calendar with industry events, awards and
  conferences.
- Research sector-specific events; e.g., if you are a
  wedding business, what are the wedding-related
  events, awards or groups you want to participate
  in? Plot these in.
- Consider generic business events for founder
  awards, marketing, design.

— Think regionally – lots of local regions have their own independent business or founder awards.

Content summary

Every business now needs to be a publisher so you need to think about the following content ideas and match them against the key dates you have created (or even use them to fill in the gaps).

It helps to first write a list of how many of these you would like to do annually, then break it down by quarter and then monthly so that you can then see a clear pattern of activity for the year.

- Guest post/article
- 'How to' guide
- Interview
- Podcast
- Live-streamed video
- Whitepaper/Research report
- Newsletter
- Press releases
- Trend pitch
- Talk/Panel event
- Other activity

For now, you can leave this blank, but you may wish to populate it with ideas from Chapters Three and Four as you work your way through the book

BONUS ACTIVITY

With all campaigns I work on, I am also thinking about the future, so I often break down my key calendar dates by long lead, mid lead and short leads.

Long lead

The one that most people might have heard of is Christmas in July. Basically, long lead refers to monthly magazines that are working six months in advance. No good going to *Vogue* in January to pitch your perfect product for a New Year's Resolution; you should be doing that in August.

If you have photography of your product or an event image you can use six months ahead then you are good to go and it's definitely worth marking in your calendar when to start pitching.

Mid lead

Similar to the above, but for me, mid leads are 6–8 weeks (usually this can differ for different titles) – this is more applicable to the *Time Out* magazine-type publications. If you are planning an event, launch, or something that is timing-specific, then working far in advance is essential, so you have time to craft and issue your press materials ahead of the launch.

Short lead

Typically, short leads are your online publications. But again, even with them you want to be giving them a heads up of at least a week in advance. No good pitching someone your fantastic Valentine's Day stunt on the day. And I think it's always better to be safe than sorry. In my opinion, you can never be pitching your event, service or activity too early – someone can always say come back. But if you are too late, the opportunity is dead.

EXAMPLE

	January	February	March	April	May	June
Key business dates						
National days – SL						
National days – ML						
National days – LL						
Awards/ conferences						
Content						
Other activity						
	July	August	September	October	November	December
Key business dates						
National days – SL						
National days – ML						
National days – LL						
Awards/ conferences						
Content						
Other activity						

TIPS

- Make sure you plan in advance where necessary (e.g., if you want to pitch to long-lead magazines or pitch to speak at a conference) to make sure the things that need a lot of consideration are included.
- If thinking ahead for a full 12 months is too much, then start with monthly or quarterly content.
- At the beginning of each month, I write a week-by-week plan to ensure I am keeping my strategy on track.
- Sit and review your calendar at least monthly to make sure you are on track – schedule a monthly communications planning meeting with yourself/ your key stakeholders and cross-reference against your objectives to make sure you are staying on brand.

1.7 Crisis Q&A

When you put your business out there, it doesn't matter how big the spotlight is. There are going to be people who like you and some who do not. With the age of social media, people can even share their disdain for you in a very public forum and the trick with this is not to react emotionally.

Your current customers are your most valuable asset and you should spend just as much time serving them, if not more so, than trying to acquire the next customer. So being prepared is important. With this in mind, it is a good idea to prepare some crisis communication materials in advance.

ACTIVITY

Particularly for customer-centric businesses, I would highly recommend creating a crisis Q&A crib sheet. This does not have to be a huge document but think about the sort of criticism you might face; e.g.,

- Your product was lost in the post.
- It didn't look like what was advertised.
- Somebody felt like they received bad service from you.

In the heat of the moment, the worst thing that you can do is to ostrich. With a crisis document in place, whilst you don't want to give robotic responses, you have a framework to base your answers.

TIPS

- Whilst almost everything I have suggested in this book is for you to hype yourself for free, booking some one-to-one coaching or seeking some training in crisis response could be beneficial to pre-empt any disasters.
- Don't just ignore customers' or journalists' requests for a response.
- Update your social media as soon as information is available.

Chapter summary

So, if you have completed all the above tasks can you clearly tick off the items below?

- Do you have defined business objectives that you are happy with?
- Are you clear on your communications objectives?
- Have you mapped out your audience?
- Do you know everything about your audience and what they are consuming?
- Have you cross-referenced your USP against your competitors' to make sure that the language is not the same, and that it can only apply to you?
- Have you created an annual communications calendar with your key dates for the year for activation?
- Have you ensured you have a framework in place for customer complaints?

You may now be wondering why you have already got this far and worked this hard and I've not even told you how to do any actual PR yet. By looking at the checklist above, I hope you now have a well-thought-through blueprint with clearer directions for where your business is heading. The work in this chapter is essential for you to have strong foundations to execute your communications strategically.

And don't hate me, but you still have got to get through another quarter of the book doing work on yourself before I'll let you out the gate. But it *will* be worth it, I promise. Once you start thinking about your business in this way you will start to spot opportunities for yourself out there. Let me know how you are getting on via social media and get rolling your sleeves up for Chapter 2. Because if you want to hype yourself faster, we've got work to do.

CHAPTER 2

MASTER YOUR MEDIA TOOLKIT

This chapter is a media toolkit guide 101. It's everything you need before you speak to media, event organisers, brand partners, sponsorship or collaborators. I want to get you thinking about all the essentials you need for pitching. If you need help driving awareness, sales or want to start building your credibility as an industry expert then this chapter is essential for you.

Whether you use OneDrive, Dropbox, Google Drive or your desktop (but please don't do that!), you should have a folder called press or media toolkit where you save all the documents that you need for your press and marketing purposes and you should update them regularly. When these documents are requested, to make the journalist's job easier and to increase your chances of coverage, you need to be able to access these easily.

So, this chapter will walk you through all the elements I recommend you have before your hype machine starts, including:

- One-liner
- Boiler plates
- Images
- Biographies
- Thought topics
- Feature topics
- Press release.

And yes, I put the press release last because it serves as a useful reminder that the press release is *not* the most essential part of your media toolkit.

2.1 One-liner

This is where the work you have done on yourself in Chapter 1 is going to come into play. For book research, I've gone to a big bunch of networking events, panel talks and listened to a *lot* of podcasts. I tell you who I remember – the people who tell me what they do clearly and concisely.

If someone can't summarise what they do, I often only remember them by thinking, Gosh – you were boring. Nailing your summary sentence is a key skill and it should roll off the tongue. Just like you know the hospital you were born in, your date of birth and your mother's maiden name, you need to be able to reel off what your business does with confidence in a pithy way.

ACTIVITY

- Think about how you would chat to a friend; how do you describe what your business does in one sentence?
- If you are struggling, write down a paragraph to explain what your business does but then draft – chop out all unnecessary words by bringing out that red pen again.
- Does it leave room for people to ask questions (but it's not a necessity)?

EXAMPLE

One sentence case study – The Good

I've included a few of my favourites that are out in the wild because I feel that not only do they say what it is the business does, but leave room for further intrigue and questions.

"Poopy Cat are fun disposable litter trays that are better for you, better for the cat and better for the environment."

"With the Karma App, you can find delicious unsold food from restaurants and enjoy at half the regular price."

"We're a retail brand selling smart tech to busy people. Clever stuff that solves problems. Because useful is the new cool." (Soda Says)

One sentence case study – The Bad

Below are some examples that don't work with my made-up business, The ZZ.

"The ZZ is a collective of creative talent, specialising in disruption."

This is so broad, and I have to read it several times to realise I still don't know what this means. What type of creative talent? Specialising in disruption, OK, so maybe you might be an innovation business? I literally don't know if you are mischief makers at Paddy Power who create quirky stunts or people who make quirky protest signs.

"A XX, for everybody."

I always get worried when brands claim they are for everyone. Firstly, because honing in on a niche always seems more sensible; and secondly, because their advertising and promotional materials don't always show that. So, unless you are reflecting everybody in your materials, then don't do it.

TIPS

- Your one-liner is different to your USP, it is what I call the "Ronseal plus intrigue" to describe what it is your brand does.
- Have you explained your business so a five-year-old would understand?

- Keep it super simple, I'm looking for 10–12 words here *max*, people.
- Can you leave an element of curiosity, so people want to know more?
- It's OK if your one sentence evolves over time as your business pivots. Great one-liners stop you in your tracks and leave you wanting more.
- Check all your social media accounts and your website – are you using the same information across all platforms?

2.2 Boiler plate

The Cambridge dictionary describes the boiler plate as "writing that has been used before many times with only very small changes". The term originates from the early 1900s when printing plates of text for widespread production were cast or stamped in steel. Today, it isn't for a whole press release or stories but what I would call your business biography, the equivalent of the 'about us' column.

It should look like a potted history of your business and is information that rarely changes. It is used at the bottom of your press release, but increasingly I use the boiler plate as part of my hype pitches.

ACTIVITY

Imagine you are in a pub (you can have a soft drink or a pint, I'm not here to judge) – I want you to tell your mate what your business does in one paragraph. Write it down and make sure it covers the following:

- What actually *is* your business? You need a brief statement on what you do and the name of your business.
- Where does your business do this and since when?
- Who established the business and for what purpose?
- Any notable business successes to highlight?

TIPS

- Keep this short, sharp and succinct.
- Show it to someone who doesn't know anything about your business and make sure that they can read it and understand what your business does.
- Cut out any words or language you don't need.
- This should be a factual, pithy marketing paragraph so avoid opinionated or emotive language.

CHECKLIST

- Check all your social media accounts and your website – are you using the same information across all platforms?
- Ask that mate down the pub again (you can go to the coffee shop now if you need to, supporting a local business is an ace idea though) to listen

to your boiler plate and one-liner, get some feedback.
- Are you part of any networking groups on Facebook/LinkedIn that you can get some additional feedback from?

2.3 Images

If you take nothing else from this book, I hope you spend some time working on your biography and investing in some professional photography. With great photography you instantly elevate your personal and business brand.

For me, these are the non-negotiable parts of a press office and I wouldn't promote a person or a business without them.

Founder images

The press shots of yourself will become the most used element in the Hype Yourself toolkit; they are essential for:

- Guest panellists at a conference
- Award entries
- Guest posts
- Updating your social media channels
- Including on your own website
- Podcast promotion.

ACTIVITY

- Make sure you work with a photographer that you feel comfortable with. All portrait photographers have a different style.
- Look around your network and ask for recommendations, it is not always about going with the cheapest photographer.
- Create a mood board of the style of photography you liked on Pinterest to share as part of the briefing process with your photographer.
- Pick a photographer who provides a briefing template or who at least sets some questions in advance of the shoot.

TIPS

- Aim for at least 6–8 headshots on plain backgrounds.
- Secure a mixture of landscape and portrait (increasingly I need to provide landscape profile pictures for blog posts/media articles).
- On shoot day wear a few outfits and in different colours.
- Consider revising every six months but *at* least once a year and try to get a mixture across the different seasons.
- Ensure you have professional cropped head and shoulder shots.
- Look directly into the camera, don't pull a funny face and try not to look too serious.

- Ask your photographer to send images to you in both hi- and low-res.
- Jpeg format is best for the majority of media/ marketing requirements.
- Make sure the shots are taken straight on, not at an angle from above/below.
- Artistic shots and full length are an added bonus.
- Top tip: outdoor shots on a beautiful sunny day will give you the best light.

Product photography

If your business is product-led, I imagine product photography will be one of the first parts of your marketing mix that you create but ensure that you consider what the media are looking for. The biggest mistake I see small businesses make is to invest heavily in over art-directed lifestyle shots, but the reality is that most media want products on a ghost or white background they can cut out easily for their shopping pages.

ACTIVITY

- Think about the pages or destination you want your product to end up in and ensure that you have a selection of shots that can be used for media.
- Don't over think your press photography, businesses are often scared of the simplicity of shooting on a plain white background, but trust me when I say that this is the most requested shot I am ever asked for.

TIPS

- Shoot your product flat lay on a white background (or what we sometimes call ghost cut-out).
- Make sure you have both low- and hi-res photography.
- The resolution should be 300 dpi – jpegs are the best format.

Business-to-business photography

If you are a service business, you might get by with generic shop-bought imagery for your website or using Unsplash for social media, but this is not going to wash for journalists.

ACTIVITY

- Everyone has seen the overused and rather dull flat lay image of a MacBook with a millennial pink notebook and a latte – so think differently, what images really represent you and your business that are not generic?
- Could you take some photos of you at work; e.g., at your desk, hosting a meeting, speaking at an event, directing a shoot? Think about all the visual aspects of what you do and how you can capture this.
- Create a bank of images (4–6) that are a mixture of portrait and lifestyle and reflect your business personality.

TIPS

- After headshots, the business 'lifestyle' shots are the ones that most companies ignore.
- If you have a physical space for your business, what can you do to make it more memorable so people might want to snap a pic and share it with their followers?

CHECKLIST

- Do you have all your photos saved in both high and low resolutions?
- Are your images captioned and labelled properly (don't just leave it saved as a numerical file — make sure you have a clear description and it is captioned.

2.4 Biographies

Whether I'm pitching a client for writing an opinion piece, speaking at an event or speaking on a podcast — inevitably the first question I will be asked (if I've not already included it as part of my pitch format) is "Can you send me their bio" and they want it immediately.

It is surprising how many businesses have been going for years where the key stakeholders don't have a biography on file when, in my opinion, this should be one of the first assets you create for your media toolkit. Or, if they do already have a bio, it tends to be a bit dull and I'm bored halfway down the list of all the professional accomplishments.

ACTIVITY

Tell me everything

Generally, entrepreneurs fall into two camps, wanting to share absolutely everything *or* fearing they don't have enough to say. To begin with, write down everything because not only is this a useful exercise to uncover all your forgotten talents and experience, but it may also unearth something different that you can build on. Ask yourself the following questions:

- What skills do you have that are relevant to this business?
- What are your relevant academic or professional qualifications?
- What is your industry experience?
- Any other strengths to highlight?
- Do you have a quirky hobby and/or habit?

The red pen

Going through all of this information, which is the most important? Rank the different points as to what are the most relevant. And start your cull of what might be irrelevant for your first draft. (Keep a long-form version of everything for future use and to keep updating.)

What's your name and where do you come from?

Cilla Black always nailed a good intro. Having read some monstrosities out there, it's worth flagging to start simply and with the basics – your name and where you currently work or some examples of who you currently work for if you are freelance.

Add a personal detail

Back to those interesting hobbies or habits. As mentioned earlier, people relate better to people who are personable so consider adding an interesting titbit. It gives the reader something to care about and might spark a wealth of opportunities.

Keep it succinct

Bonus points if you can keep it down to less than 150 words, but absolutely no more than 250. If you start putting too much information down, it actually distracts from you as an expert. You may struggle to keep it short and want to include everything but remember that people don't remember long bios, they get bored by them. You can always link to your website to encourage people to find out more.

EXAMPLE

Below is an example and some fun facts that I use to pitch Oonagh Simms, founder of The Marshmallowist. Unlike many foodie startups, Oonagh has some extremely credible food credentials which help to assert her position as an authority in her niche.

Bio

Working at the École Médéric in Paris, she endured four years of early mornings, black coffee, bake ache, 30,000 croissants, 10,000 profiteroles and finally qualified as a fully trained Pâtissièr & Chocolatier. Ready to start a new adventure she returned to London to work as a chocolatier for a leading luxury confectioner before she realised that the French style of marshmallow was missing. She became 'The Marshmallowist', creating fruit marshmallows in grown-up flavours with a French, soufflé-like texture and a signature London edge.

Fun facts

— Oonagh is a human sugar thermometer, she can tell the exact temperature of a vat of boiling sugar — just by looking at it.
— In the five weeks before Christmas, Oonagh will usually whip up 250,000 marshmallows.

- Oonagh is now so skilled at reverse parking a white van on narrow London streets that she's signed up for a stunt driving course this summer.
- Oonagh has created over 500 different flavours of marshmallows.

TIPS

- Your bio is not a one size fits all template, it will need to evolve depending on which platform or business is using it.
- Check your master biography at least once a year to ensure all recent developments are included.
- Consider having a link to download your bio and images from your website to encourage people to book you as a speaker.
- Have you also drafted the following bio options for Twitter/LinkedIn/Facebook?

CHECKLIST

- Do you have your images saved in one low-res folder and one hi-res folder?
- Do you have a link to download hi-res images that you can send out?
- Do you have a bio that is less than 150 words?
- Do you have your image and bio downloadable from your own website (you're 100% more bookable the minute you do this)?

— Have you included contact details on your bio so if someone receives it from a forwarded email chain, they can immediately contact you?

How to send out images and bios

I'm going to get into the nitty gritty of how to pitch to media in Chapter 3, but just wanted to flag a few watch outs for you now as this can often shape the briefing process:

— Don't save your images/bio as a PDF. This is because most media and editors will want access to these resources quickly and easily.
— Don't save your images/bio as a PDF attached. I know. I'm a broken record *but* I've seen it a lot.
— Attach a low-res image or include in the body of the email so journalists have a visual prompt that doesn't clog up their inbox.
— Don't send a large image to media unless requested, it clogs up their inbox and stops them being able to get important emails. You don't want to be the person that blocks their inbox.
— Cut and paste and put it in the body of an email and sometimes attach as a Word doc as an FYI so that they have all the information to hand.

2.5 Guest posts

Guest posts are often called other things such as opinion pieces, thought leadership, op-eds, blog posts or 'How to' guides. In this section, I want you to start getting the wheels turning into all the areas you could hype yourself as we progress through the book.

I could write a whole book on guest posting alone, namely because it is the *best* single-handed hype skill that I believe everyone can and should learn which works for both introverts and extroverts.

Guest posting is:

- An ace way to grow your new business leads
- Content that lives longer than an advertisement
- A free and repeatable system – once you have nailed how to do this you have endless opportunities to get your brand out there
- A stepping stone to paid-for speaking gigs
- Going to build your credibility and authority, to cement your position as an expert
- A useful mechanism to encourage sign-up to your newsletter
- A free tool to encourage social media followers
- An easy way to form part of your content creation
- A way to establish what you want to own as a business
- A great way to carve up your niche if you have multiple business owners.

All businesses are now publishers; we can see this from bigger businesses, so small businesses and entrepreneurs are agile enough to create regular and timely content without going through corporate red tape to get published.

What is the difference between an opinion piece and a thought leadership article?

An opinion piece should be just that – your own opinion. And ideally the stronger the better because if it creates debate and wider discussion you will secure a wider readership and exposure as people 'like' and comment.

A thought leadership piece can encompass opinions but is also an umbrella term for anything that shows you are a thought leader in this area, so it could be a 'How to' guide or a 'Top Tips' piece.

ACTIVITY

– *Read:* If you don't already know which industry issues are important to you then start by looking at your peers and contemporaries to see what they are saying/where they are saying it. Also, if you are anything like me, the more information you consume, the more ideas it will spark.

– *Niche:* Go back to your business objectives, target audience and media. Where are your audience? If you are a pet brand, then the obvious place is to look at pet magazines, blogs and podcasts.

But where else are the pet owners and are there specialist reports, columns or angles you can look at?

- *List build:* Start to brainstorm a list of the key areas you want to talk about and continually update and add to it. I often find that I can be reading a magazine, watching a TV programme or having a chat with friends and this sparks an idea that I'll write down. The more you can get into the habit of this the better. You can't ever have too many topic ideas. *But* you do want to stick to a few to give you an area that you are known for.
- Build a list of the titles you would like to be featured in both personally and professionally for a guest article.
- Research these titles to check if they take guest content.
- Draft ideas in the format of these publications and build a list of talking points.
- Keep all your thought leadership thinking in one place; I often have what I call brain farts, where ideas drop in unexpectedly (in fact the whole of Chapter 4 is to encourage you to think in this way).
- When it comes to pitching to media, you can pick the most relevant top three ideas from your pool for that title.

EXAMPLE

My initial response on speaking to Davinia Tomlinson, founder of Rainchq, was that I would be unable to work on a fintech product because financial services are my Achilles heel and I honestly thought her money would be better spent elsewhere.

It can be tempting when launching a new service or product to write a press release about this and expect issuing this to be the mechanism you will use to drive press coverage.

However, creating a list of talking points or opinions can be a great way to secure coverage for a new business. Dav is a great example of how you can use talking points to generate launch coverage without using a press release.

Right from the beginning I delved into Davinia's past work history and all the moments that led to her creating Rainchq. The challenges she was trying to solve with the business, included:

- For a long time, she was one of the only women, let alone a woman of colour, working in financial services.
- The negative press around financial services was putting off everyone, but particularly women, from investing.
- The current language and marketing communications used to get women to invest wasn't working.

- The women, when they did invest, were actually better at it than men, so we just had to get them started.

Davinia was a brilliant client because she wasn't afraid to Hype herself and her story to secure press coverage. By sharing her own opinions and experiences she emotionally connected with others which is what drew her audiences.

Some examples of guest post topics we used to pitch to media included:

- Financial services don't speak to women.
- Women are hurtling towards pension poverty.
- Top tips for fighting against the ethnicity pay gap.

TIPS

- Review your list of topics and ensure that they are actually a strong opinion and not what you would naturally expect.
- The more opinion pages you read, the more you will get a feel for the type of articles that do well and spark ideas for your own topics to talk about.
- Google 'submit an opinion' to get an idea of publications that take submissions and what they are looking for.
- Check our tips from opinion editor Jess Austin in Chapter 3.1.

CHECKLIST

- Do you have a list of at least three topics you can talk about professionally that will cement your position as an expert?
- Have these topics already been covered in the titles you want to be in? If so, how can you take these forward?
- What about you personally? What can you talk about?

2.6 Features

Put simply, two is a coincidence. Three is a trend. And a feature pitch is you highlighting a trend. This is where knowing your competitors can actually be a great thing. Learning to pitch a feature offers a greater chance for you to Hype Yourself than, say, just issuing news, because you can tap into multiple occasions. But you can only issue news once.

When you read any newspaper or magazine, they typically have the same format. News and more urgent shorter pieces are up front, and features tend to be around the middle. These are long-form pieces of writing that tend to quote several experts to demonstrate a trend or a debate.

Rather than pitching yourself or your company, a feature pitch can be a way of making you more relevant because telling your own brand story on its own isn't enough.

ACTIVITY

- Go back to the list of media you identified in Chapter 1.4 and ensure you are reading the feature pages of the titles you identified.
- In your workbook write down '1. Business', '2. Customers' and '3. Personal' and answer the following questions:

Business

- o Do you have any interesting HR policies in place?
- o Do you work in an unusual way?
- o Is there an alternative recruitment policy you have?
- o What is innovative and unique to how your business operates, whether that is an internal process or your go-to-market proposition?

Customers

- o What is interesting about your audience?
- o Have you noticed a behavioural change or anything interesting about your audience?
- o Have you had to adapt your offering or product to meet customer demand?

Personal

- o What is interesting about your personal journey? Have you had to overcome adversity to create your business?

- Do you have an unusual lightbulb moment?
- Do you work with a twin, a best friend, an ex, your grandparents or is there something unusual or unique about your business set-up?

NB: To the uninitiated, thinking about what can be interesting for a feature can be difficult, so I've included lots of examples in the following section; this is an area that does come with time or you may want to source some one-to-one coaching or assistance to help develop your ideas.

EXAMPLE

Below are six different feature types you may spot in the wild:

1. *Trends:* a recent example of this is the rise of 'cleanfluencers'; off the back of the Marie Kondo show, there have been several articles on people who are cleaning influencers, or the top cleaning/home tidying products.

   Or the coverage generated on cannabidiol (CBD) wellness features for The Marshmallowist and their limited-edition CBD mallows.

2. *Seasonal features:* throughout the calendar, you can guarantee that just like the seasons there will be recurrent themes for features that appear. At Christmas you may see a feature on businesses who make their living from this time of year.

Or increasingly, I've spotted a lot of 'End of Year Teacher Gifting' features that look at gifts for this time of year.

3. *Getting personal:* people with unusual backgrounds, hobbies or achievements can make interesting stories. Try to create ideas that resonate on a human level; who are the characters of your story and do they fit a particular profile? If you have statistics and research can you provide a case study that provides an emotive connection?

4. *New consumer behaviour:* the rise of subscriptions, the death of the high street, veganism, the Internet of Things (IoT) in the home – are examples of features on types of consumer behaviour we have seen over the years.

5. *Data:* your customer data, shopping habits or behaviour change statistics have potential for national or trade press coverage. Great examples of customer data might include shopping peaks after a cultural event or item in the news *or* identify a surprising new trend.

6. *Trade features:* a quick and simpler way than pitching your own feature idea is to contribute to an already existing feature. Trade magazines such as *The Grocer* have Forward Feature lists. These break down the topics they are planning to cover, so when I knew they were writing a piece on functional drinks, it was an opportunity to pitch comments from my

client MOJU, which resulted in more coverage and awareness about their new triple ginger shot range than a stand-alone press release.

We are not going to talk about how to craft the email for a feature pitch in this section but just as you have whittled down topics for talking points, it is good for you to start thinking in the same way about feature angles.

TIPS

- What significant dates or consumer behaviour does your business have access to?
- Do you think you have created a market first or are you part of an emerging new category?
- Can you use business data from the City Business Library, for example, or look at Trade Associations to find recent reports and statistics that can support a wider contextual piece that your business could fit into?
- Look at the feature and trend articles in local newspapers to get a feel for the topics being covered.

CHECKLIST

- Next time you are reading a magazine/paper have a look through; who are the features writers and what are the trends you are spotting?
- Make sure you are thinking ahead for features and plotting in advance in your calendar. No

good pitching a Christmas feature in December, for example.
- Don't duplicate a feature you have already seen – how can you take the subject forward?

2.7 Press releases

To reinforce notes from earlier in this book, Hyping Yourself does not mean writing a press release and issuing it to a media list. Part of my negativity towards press releases is due to many business owners (and even some PRs) thinking that publicity is about writing a press release and issuing it to a database of contacts. This is wrong because it is actually lazy and sloppy, like cold-calling a business to sell to them without knowing a single thing about them and if your product or service is useful.

I would always recommend writing a press release because it provides crucial background information for a journalist to write an informed article, but it is how you use the press release to pitch that is the most essential lesson here. So, I'm going to teach you the basics of crafting a press release, but for the love of God, don't issue it without getting through Chapter 3.

To be clear, a press release should be a one- or two-page document that shares your business's breaking news. When issued correctly to journalists they can be crucial for driving media coverage, building brand awareness and are a cost-effective way to market your business. It is just your time that is involved.

ACTIVITY

In your notebook or computer, you can have a go at writing your first press release by following the instructions below. If you own a product or service business, it can be worth keeping a press release on file that explains what you do as a background document for practice or incase a journalist requests one.

Headlines

Make sure you use an attention-grabbing headline. It can include a pun, but make sure it's clear what it is about. Think about the headlines of articles in the paper when you read them: check your headline for readability using a tool like 'headline analyser'. Successful headlines draw you in. Your headline must do the same.

Date and location

Include your location and the date that the press release is being issued for.

Intro paragraph

Your opening paragraph should contain the five Ws:

- – Who is this story about?
- – What is happening?
- – Where is it going on?

— When will it occur?
— Why is it important?

The first paragraph should set the scene and tone for the whole press release. You have the headline, and then the first paragraph is your opening for setting the story. It should be very clear what the newshook is within this paragraph.

Paragraphs two to five

These should include the other details of your story in a descending order of importance. For now, keep all information about when you were founded, what you do, team biographies, and other factual information out of the press release. That isn't to say that the rest of your release shouldn't be factual; it absolutely must be factual and can't be biased. The next several paragraphs should tell the complete story concisely with important supporting details included.

Style: other things to watch out for

Make sure you don't have too much jargon or things that only mean something to your industry. Write as if an intelligent five-year-old could understand what it is you're talking about. If you are not sure, ask a friend (they don't need to be a clever child) if they understand what you are saying. If they find it boring or complicated, ditch your jargon.

Quotes

Whether it is a business or consumer story, include a quote from the CEO/founder to give context. Watch out for the following statements, however:

- "I am delighted."
- "I am excited."
- "We can't wait for ..."

They are the most clichéd and overused quotes – and who actually talks like that?

Your quote needs to be bold. Make sure the quote gives a purpose. It is your opportunity to give more colour or opinion and can be really personal. This is where you can say how you really feel, so make it memorable.

Make sure you attribute the quote, who is saying what and why.

Press contact

At the bottom of your press release, be sure to include contact information – your name, email and a phone number. The phone number is key, particularly if time is of the essence and a journalist needs to be able to fact check. Key URLs and social media handles should also be shared here.

Editors' Notes

Key prices, dates, event information or any other information that can be included in listicle format.

Boiler plate

The boiler plate you crafted earlier should sit right at the bottom of your press release.

EXAMPLES

Head to the Press Release example template from www.thewern.com/book; this provides a framework and plenty of examples, but I've outlined below a few instances where you might want to consider writing a press release.

Examples of when you might want to issue a press release include:

- Breaking news announcements
- Events
- Partnerships or collaborations
- Product launches or limited editions
- Sharing research
- Announcing award wins of senior hires
- Crisis management.

TIPS

- If your business isn't well known, maybe consider not using it for your headline and think instead what the headline of the story might be.
- The press release should be written in the same style as a news article – in that the news is right up top and in front and the supporting background information comes further down.
- Don't overdo it – avoid overuse of exclamation marks, fluffy language or wild claims; e.g., the World's First or Best New Product for XX.
- Keep background information in Editors' Notes: see Chapter 3 for pop-ups and the Blondies Kitchen pop-up release for what I mean.

Sarah Drumm freelance journalist and formerly Courier Media's News Editor adds:

A press release is always helpful but a bespoke pitch that sums up the story succinctly is best. If I know you have also only sent the story to me that is also good, so when sending me a press release include a brief note on what the story is, which section of the magazine it fits into and flag if it hasn't gone elsewhere. To get me to open the email in the first place, if you are an unknown business maybe don't include your company name in the subject line but explain what the story is."

CHECKLIST

- Have you done a spelling and grammar check?
- Make sure you can totally understand the crux of your story with just the first paragraph and keep it to less than one side of A4.
- Have you kept longer factual information for the Editors' Notes section at the bottom?
- Did you include your contact information, email and phone number and boiler plate?
- Keep it short and to the point and avoid fluffy language.

Chapter summary

Congratulations, you are now at the halfway point. If you are more of a creative or go-getter, the next half is for you and this first bit may have been a bit tough. But trust me when I say that this planning work will already put your business miles ahead of other small businesses and even many of those businesses who are not using quality PR agencies.

Through my work with The Wern, I'm consistently shocked when I consult for other companies only to discover that when I ask them for this information to go to media with, they don't have any of it.

Having now completed the first chapters, you should have done some deeper strategic thinking within Chapter

I which enables you to write your press materials in this chapter. The preparation in this chapter will mean you are now ready to start pitching and able to respond to inbound requests.

If you have a press office toolkit, you should now also have:

- One-liner
- Boiler plate
- USP
- Images
- Biography
- A list of topics for thought leadership
- A list of topics for features
- A skeleton of what your press release should look like.

CHAPTER 3

STARTING YOUR PRESS OFFICE

If Chapters One and Two were the theory test, then Chapters Three and Four are the practical sessions. The work in the first two chapters was essential for your communications blueprint and foundation of your PR campaign.

In this chapter, I'm going to cover off the following topics:

- How to build your media database
- How you can build your relationships with media
- How to pitch out a product
- How to pitch out a service
- How to get on a podcast
- How to speak on a panel
- How to host an event
- Opportunities for TV
- Opportunities for radio
- Business Q&As.

And hold fire for Chapter 4 to really wet your whistle on creative ideas.

NB: It is worth remembering that even if you are a service-based business, you might want to consider creating a product or vice versa to be able to promote what it is you do under another guise.

3.1 Journalist details

Your journalist database is your Bible when it comes to media relations and should form the backbone of any press office. OK. Firstly, we know that I do like to complain about people who ask me about my Rolodex or black book of contacts (Hello 90s stationery, I'll just get my Filofax out at the same time shall I?). The reason this gets my back up is because I know that a good publicist should be able to pitch a story to a stranger and make it land. If you are telling your story well and can demonstrate that you understand their readership and why the story is compelling to their readers, listeners or viewers, this whole 'needing to be armed with contacts' feels archaic.

The best publicists I have worked with aren't the ones with contacts, they are the ones who are passionate about telling the story and taking the time to craft it right rather than rushing it.

However, with that said, it is *of course* worth starting with your own network to see if you have any contacts you can make the most of.

Joe Makertich, former editor of *ShortList* adds:

> Find out if you have any friends or friends of
> friends who work in journalism. And then find a
> way to talk to them without making it feel forced
> or annoying. There's always a way. Tell them your
> story. As long as it's concise and effective they
> will, at the very least, remember it for a while.
> They might well know someone to approach, or
> even be in the middle of something you can help
> out with (I'd often meet up with old friends I'd
> not seen for ages and end up incorporating them
> into some feature).

This isn't about quantity – *repeat* – you don't want a
list of 100. You want the titles that fit your needs and
consider that you might also want to speak to a few
different desks.

ACTIVITY

I always start with a blank spreadsheet and go shopping.
Read the magazine and pull out all the areas that are
relevant to your business. This is what we call 'tear
sheets' – I assume this is because we tear them out. I
have a folder with different sections; e.g., products for
interior, products for food and drink, app columns,
business interviews.

I take those torn-out sheets and input them to a
spreadsheet. If you don't like Excel, you can use a table in

whatever program you like, but generally, these are the columns I would say you need:

- first name
- surname
- publication
- job title
- name of column
- email
- background information
- social media handles
- specific notes to know
- title of sell-in
- phone number – although as a general rule of thumb, don't phone them.

Twitter

You should by now have the right name of the journalist you need; as a first port of call I often check Twitter as this often reveals how they want to be contacted and a contact address or website. If you 100% know they cover your beat, you can also DM them for information.

Telephone

For niche publications, it is perfectly acceptable to phone the switchboard and ask for the spelling format of the title or a particular person. Nationals and bigger titles can't always do this, but if you get really stuck it is always worth an ask.

The website of the publication

For me this is the most obvious one; as Jeremy Carson, Founder of FitKit has always sought his own press coverage, he adds: "The contact details of the journalists at the Grocer were easy to come by as they're on the editorial list page of the magazine with contact numbers. It's easier than people think to speak to the right people."

And he raises a good point, speaking to the *right* person is key. Many stories go to the publicity graveyard not because they are crap, but because they went to the wrong person (take my example of Trint above).

Media databases

If you look at the business desk of *The Times*, for example, on my media database there are 23 different journalists. 23! If I send it to the wrong one, I can't rely on them forwarding it to the right person. It is for this reason alone that I don't think media databases are often worth the investment for small businesses, freelancers or entrepreneurs. That said, if you are using it to just cross-reference a name or quickly search a contact, they can be a brilliant tool. Many offer packages where you can split the costs with other small businesses. I had an argument with a salesman recently who told me my thinking was bizarre. He couldn't understand how me paying £5k a year for his service couldn't possibly save me time and money. But my argument was that a list of email addresses is worth nothing. The reason I get great coverage is because I take my time to send bespoke pitches to journalists and if I have a media database, how do I know who out of the 23 business journalists is the right one without taking time to do the desk research? They are expensive, often out of date and they encourage bad practice. Remember *one* size fits *no one*.

In print

I really hope by now I've banged the drum enough that you are buying the publications you want to be in. When you look inside many of these, usually on the inside sleeve or on the bespoke pages there will be the contact details.

Media enquiry databases

It is often worth having a trial of PressPlugs, ResponseSource, JournoLink or Gorkana when you are starting out to get an idea of the sort of different desks and sheer number of journalists that there are. It also gives you an idea of the sort of hidden costs PR freelancers/agencies have as we are all usually subscribed to at *least* one of these in order to be able to do our job. But also, any journalists who are relevant you can save into your spreadsheet for when it is relevant.

EXAMPLE

Most of these titles are self-explanatory, but some are more crucial than others and I'll explain why.

Background information. So, a tiny bit of perfectly respectable stalking goes on here. Don't be creepy, though! I just mean Googling them to see what other articles they've written. Is there a theme to the types of stories they write?

Maybe they have written about a competitor or a similar topic. Include the link to the article in your background information. Get to know them.

Include their Twitter handle. You don't have to be posting all the time, but as a gold mine for journalist information and breaking news, I would thoroughly recommend having a Twitter account but do see what sorts of things interest them. They may even provide tips on the types of stories they are looking for or how to pitch to them.

Title of sell-in. You might go to the same journalists about more than one story. So, each time I'm pitching out a new story, I create a new column. Let's say in this instance, the story is, "App launch". This would be my header, and then I put the date and notes: "12/02 –Lucy pitched on email for the 'App of the Week' column. No feedback as of yet."

This way, if you get a response, coverage or feedback, you can log into one place with it all together. This helps because you may then think, "Well, it's been two weeks, and I've had no feedback, so now I'm going to send one email to follow up or try a different angle to see if this works".

Unless you have a photographic memory of your sent items, having this spreadsheet will keep your pitching organised.

Telephone numbers. A word of caution here: the jury is out on whether to phone a journalist or not. In my experience, I try not to phone unless it is particularly newsworthy and relevant for that day.

TIPS

In this section I've asked a few journalists to talk about their roles and how to pitch to them. But there are *loads* of events where you can meet journalists/hear them talk and my biggest tip is get to know the sort of writers you want to be approaching before you learn *how* to approach them.

Different types of journalists

I always tell anybody looking to self-PR to start with just *five* journalists and study them. Every journalist works in a different way, with a different editorial interest regardless of their job description, but I thought that being aware of some of the different roles might give you some insight into the sort of journalist you might need to be pitching for. Below, I've asked a few to contribute but there are hundreds of different types and it is up to you to do due diligence on what the right sort of journalist for you might look like.

Opinion editor
This is a very niche role – we asked Jess Austin from *Metro* to explain her position:

> [M]y job varies slightly from reporters in that my role is largely to commission and edit. I very rarely write my own opinion and I am far more interested in sourcing unique voices to write on the back of news stories or share their personal stories.
>
> Every morning I look at the main stories of the day and try and find people with expertise or unique takes on these topics to write. This doesn't have to be breaking news and can be anything from a fresh angle on last night's *Love Island* to a first-person account from struggling to cope with Universal Credit. Once these are commissioned, I spend the rest of the day contacting writers for longer term projects, editing pieces and planning for upcoming news events.

Commercial content editor
If you want to work with a writer to co-create aid for content, one of the ways that you can look to secure content directly without trying to pitch editorially is working with a commercial content editor. This is a paid-for partnership between yourself and the brand and prices range for print and digital.

Rebecca Denne, Commercial Content Editor and Consultant, former Acting Head of Content at The Stylist Group says:

> The cost of commercial content varies depends on so many factors – the channel(s) you want it to run on, the distribution, the amount of budget you have for amplification, productions costs and often how much creative ownership you want to retain. For example, does the brand need a shoot, will talent be involved, with it be on location, how big will the crew be? My role as Acting Head of Content involved brands coming to my team (and others) with a brief. This would often include their objectives, assets and other mandatories – so the channels they wanted to run on or the length of time they wanted their campaign to run for. My job was to help answer their business objectives with both a journalistic and commercial hat on.

But, Rebecca warns, brand partnerships need to be authentic in order to be effective.

> You can't just do a branded piece of content and hope for the best. The brand has to be a good fit for the readership or it can turn people away from both the publication and the brand itself. The idea of co-branded content is that you are in collaboration. So, loyal readers of a publication will see your brand doing content with them, like a co-branded digital article for example and this immediately creates

an affinity for your audience which can help build brand engagement, kudos and (hopefully) sales.

Freelance writer

Kate Hollowood is a freelance writer for publications and brands including It's Nice That, Ace & Tate and Monzo. She's especially interested in creativity, mental health and money, but also writes about her local area for I Love Chatsworth Road magazine.

This means she has many hats on, but also straddles a partial role of the PR in that she also has to pitch her own stories to commissioning editors. Therefore, sending a press release to a freelance writer is unlikely to get picked up unless they write news and it's a crucial breaking news story.

Kate gives her tips on what she is looking for as a freelance writer:

> Fit the bill. It sounds obvious, but don't get in touch unless your case study fits the journalist's requirements. If they say they're looking for a vegan in their 60s, don't send them a case study about a 21-year-old. The criteria journalists describe in a callout is most often strict, so don't waste your time if you can't meet it.
>
> Stand out in your initial email to the journalist, firstly explain how your case study fits the requirements they are looking for. Then include a few sentences about how your case study is

uniquely interesting. Is your vegan the son of two cattle farmers? Have they changed their diet later in life due to an illness? Are they based in the Outer Hebrides? The journalist will likely be sifting through lots of options and so explaining why your case study is a juicy one will help your email stick out.

Flattery gets you nowhere. I've found that when I put callouts for case studies I need for Monzo, a start-up bank, people often respond telling me how much they love the brand or how the bank has 'changed their life'. This is not useful. It's understandable why they'd assume I want to hear that, but branded content is about telling an interesting story rather than shouting about how amazing the company is. If the article were to be overly self-congratulatory, it would feel inauthentic and sound just like a traditional advert. So, don't worry too much about the brand – just focus on what the journalist has asked for.

Staff writer
Kathryn Wheeler is staff writer at *Happiful* magazine; she explains to me what her role means.

I write across all sections of the magazine, from features to news, as well as online pieces – and I also write the weekly newsletter. Because I work so broadly across the magazine, the main thing that I'm looking for from pitches is that they are offering something that I couldn't already do myself, or don't have time to do myself. This may be because the person pitching is an expert in their field, or because they have great contacts and are able to bring an exclusive angle to a topic.

For pitches to the print magazine, strong imagery is incredibly important – it can be the difference between a piece making it through or not. So again, if this is something that has already been thought of – with photographer's credit, captions where necessary (identifying people, dates, etc.) and high-res print-ready files – already sorted, this is going to save the team and I a lot of time and is therefore a lot more attractive.

Digital writer
Sarah Orme tells us about all things digital:

I'm the digital editor for calmmoment.com, the online home of *In The Moment* magazine and *Project Calm*. In my role, I'm responsible for creating interesting wellbeing articles, running our social media accounts, creating email newsletters and presenting the *In The Moment* magazine podcast. I'm always trying to create interesting articles that cover our key topics: wellbeing, mindfulness, living, creating and escaping. While I don't tend to post product reviews or roundups, I'm always looking for people who have expertise in a wellness-related field who are happy to share their knowledge with our readers. If you're thinking of sending me a pitch, I would suggest spending a little time on our website first to check that we haven't already covered it. If it's something that we have already done, then we're unlikely to cover it again unless you're approaching the subject in a very different way. I really like it when people have done their research and approach me with potential article ideas that they might be able to help with. Please don't send me pre-written articles, it's much quicker and easier to send ideas!

News editor
Sarah Drumm, a freelance journalist whose most recent staff role was as Courier Media's news editor, tells us:

News editors pretty much do what's said on the tin. We are looking for stories that are new, exciting and have an element of urgency around them. News editors and reporters sometimes have the reputation that they are hunting for scandals and missteps – and, of course, these stories are important for our readers to hear if reported on constructively and responsibly – but we are equally keen to hear from companies who have launched exciting innovations, overhauled their business models, or overcome a huge challenge.

At *Courier* specifically, I had two main areas of responsibility as our news editor. First, I set the agenda for our weekly email newsletter, Courier Weekly. Each week I needed five brand new stories, so was always on the hunt for new products and interesting company announcements. Every story had to pass the timeliness test: in other words, why is it essential that this story is told *now*?

Second, I curated, edited and wrote content for the Now section of the magazine, which is the first thing readers turn to and features a mixture of short, snappy stories on various subjects relevant to the 'modern business' beat. In this section not only would we need to justify the place of every story by proving its timeliness, we also needed to make sure we had compelling images, stats or pull-quotes to draw readers in.

Editor

We spoke to former editor of *ShortList*, Joe Makertich, about the role of editor and how to approach it as well as his tips from years of experience at the top:

The role of editor depends on who you ask. The role is what you make it. In my experience it's the opportunity to work with people more interesting than myself. I get such a kick out of that aspect of it. Giving work to illustrators, journalists, designers, photographers and novelists makes me feel better about not having any talent in those areas.

It's also rewarding. Being able to spot potential in someone, or helping them realise their forte, is a crucial part of the job.

The best editors also manage to imbue their publication with a singular tone. A vibe that's their own. They do this not by micromanaging every aspect of the production (although sometimes this is tempting) but by enabling each member of staff. Once each member of staff, no matter how junior, feels valued by the editor, the publication begins to sing.

Unfortunately, a lot of non-PRs come to editors in the first instance and the chances of a stranger cold-calling me about something and it turning out that their thing was relevant or useful to me were zero.

You find the right writer by working out who your story is relevant to. Publications and brands tell stories. *Take a Break* tells different stories to *How to Spend It*, but they're all stories. And good stories all need interest/drama/jeopardy.

Ultimately every publication works in a different way. So, in some places it would be in your interests to go straight to staff writers and try and build a relationship. In other places it would be the features editor or front-section editor. In an ideal world you'd know the way each publication functioned. Who commissions who? Where do the ideas come from? Who's the person in constant need of stories/people/products?

Broadcast contacts

Firstly, let me introduce you to a few industry terms and job titles to help you with who you are looking for:

Presenter
OK, you probs know what this means, they are the people who present the show. But this does not mean this is the person you should be pitching to. The presenter's role is just that, to present. They do not get involved with the production and creation of the show's content. So, leave them in peace.

Forward planner
Many of the bigger TV shows have a forward planner. Their job titles are also a bit Ronseal in that they help to forward plan the show's content. There will be certain segments (the more magazine-type content) that can be planned in advance; e.g., every news programme tends to have a soft/'feel good' story at the end that is topical so if you know that you are launching something lovely on a particular day it is worth pitching in advance. But this applies equally for the roundup product sections of the shows. As a general rule of thumb, I might send a note to forward planners a few weeks in advance to get in the diary, and then perhaps follow up the week before to

give them a heads up of the story I am working on to see if it fits any slots they have that week. In many instances, the forward planning desk or just planning desk is who you want to be sending speculative pitches to. Forward planning and planners are usually the first go-to if you have a news pitch or are pitching yourself as an expert to comment on something topical.

Digital producer

A lot of producers for the TV stations have specific titles; e.g., digital producer means the person who is responsible for creating content for social channels associated with the show and in fact might even create a completely different bunch of content to the television show.

Demo producer

The person whose responsibility it is to source products that will be demoed on the show, usually for the lifestyle section.

Celebrity bookers

If you are lucky enough to have a well-known and topical celebrity who is fronting your campaign you may very well want to pitch your story to a celebrity booker who is charged with inviting stars to appear for 'on the sofa'-type pieces.

Beauty/fashion producer

If you have a beauty or fashion product, you could do worse than to make contact with either the beauty or fashion producers of the shows you wish to appear on.

Due to data protection laws, I can't just hand over contact details of specific journalists but below I have included some handy information that is already in the public domain to help you with your broadcast press outreach.

Planners/forward planners

If you do a Google search for "forward planner for [insert name of show]", Google will usually pull up the right page you need; e.g., if you wanted to be on the *Today* programme on Radio 4, I would Google "forward planning for the today programme" and the contact page is one of the first to appear.

Regional news

NB: this information is available on the ITV press centre website. The general ITV news is for national stories only. They do not pass on stories to regions, so if you have a regional story ensure you are contacting your relevant regional desk.

For BBC Television, you can phone the BBC switchboard (020 8743 8000) and ask to be put through to Forward Planning. This is one of the rare occasions where phoning can be acceptable and, in this instance, it is so you can find contact information.

If you have a genuinely interesting story that will add value on a nationwide scale, you can contact them with your story on: haveyoursay@bbc.co.uk

3.2 Why help a journalist who isn't directly related to your business?

Firstly, in case I've not stressed it already, there are not enough business profile columns and slots for all the brilliant businesses out there. We buy into people over the business. So finding opportunities or jumping on the bandwagon of a journalist request is a great way to practise your media relations skills.

ACTIVITY

If you want to just get a feel for what journalist requests look like, consider a trial with someone like ResponseSource, PressPlugs or JournoLink. This will help you to determine whether or not there is value in this kind of service for you and your business.

Search #journorequest on Twitter which has a constant live feed on latest requests from media looking for case studies and PRs.

LIGHTBULB is a fantastic Facebook group run by Charlotte Fall that is for entrepreneurs and journalists to connect directly (it is not for marketing or PR reps). There are many journalist requests here and you can directly speak with media.

Follow journalists on LinkedIn (without having to connect with them).

EXAMPLE

I recently noticed a journalist request for *The Times*, it was for some sponsored content by Dell on the lessons you learnt building your startup. I pitched an IT problem I had faced of having not sorted out a paid-for storage solution. I sent it in a timely manner, included my biography and a one-liner on my business alongside my photo. I didn't plug a single element of me, my work or what my business does in the piece – merely flagged a business lesson I had learnt that others could learn from.

The benefits of taking the time to pitch this meant that:

- As it was sponsored content, anyone who follows *The Times* on LinkedIn/Facebook was repeatedly seeing my face next to an article about business challenges.
- I was also the lead image on *The Times* homepage which made many people in my extended network contact me to see how I was doing.
- I received multiple business connection requests on LinkedIn and two new leads from businesses which resulted in me selling two one-to-one PR coaching packages right before I went on maternity leave.
- It means I now have had communication with a business journalist who may be of relevance to me in the future.

As another example, I contributed to an article in *Forbes* on how my partner now works with me to spend more time with our children. If you now Google my name, this is one of the first articles that appears. Although not directly related to my business, it was a great relationship builder with not only the journalist Annie Ridout, but the subjects of the other case studies included within the piece.

TIPS

There are some definite guidelines for responding to a journalist request, whether it comes from Twitter, LinkedIn or a paid-for service like PressPlugs or ResponseSource.

- Make sure you are fully answering the brief and don't try to shoehorn; e.g., if someone is asking for female twins who are tall that are vegans, don't pitch twins who are boys or are short or have a gluten allergy
- Give them everything at once – people on Twitter responding to #journorequest are the worst for this, they just say, "I've got something perfect, here is my email". No, *just no*. The journalist is busy, hence the urgent request because they need someone to contribute or be a case study. Don't make them do more work.
- The likelihood is that many PRs' business owners are spotting the same journalist request as you, so time is of the essence, you want to be one of the first to respond because if the first replies hit the mark, they are unlikely to read any of the others.

- Include your biography, one-liner on your business and a photograph so that they know you are serious, have your information prepared and will be a reliable resource.
- If you get featured, give them a thank you, this is *free* exposure for you and it's a great way to maintain your relationship.

Joe Makertich, former editor of *ShortList*, gives his tips for emails:"The best people know how to word an email, so it didn't seem intrusive or dunderheaded. Journalists could glance at it and get how its contents could help them in the near future".

In an absolutely ideal world, the PR would get some kind of email alert saying "X journalist has just been given the impossible job of writing a ten page article about rain in one week" and you'd send them an email in that instant, saying "Right, I can put you in touch with an umbrella entrepreneur who'll explain why wooden handles are overrated, a meteorologist who can list his top five weather apps and a fight choreographer who'll explain why all action scenes look cooler in the rain". That would be ideal. Ultimately good journalists will be coming to you because they want to tell a particular type of story. Is it an underdog story? A crazy story? A story of persistence? A funny story? If you make their lives easier and help them tell that story (without misreporting the truth), they'll stick with you for life.

CHECKLIST

- If you want to know more about particular writers, read their online bios in the magazine or website.
- Follow them on social channels; e.g., on LinkedIn you can follow, you don't have to connect.
- Google 'meet the media' or 'meet the journalist' events.
- Have you given them absolutely everything they need in one email and kept it short and succinct?

3.3 Where to look if you have a product and how to pitch

PR 101 for a product is to get featured in product pages. These are the pages where you see multiple products on a page, some of the more popular examples include the Indy/Best, BuzzFeed or Bustle Columns, sometimes also known as listicles, where you see roundups of the 'best cleaning products' or 'alternative advent calendars'.

Many of the business owners I work with task PR with driving sales through product placement coverage. We spoke with Jo Tutchener-Sharp, founder of Scamp & Dude (and former PR agency owner) who has a good heads up on this.

If a key business driver for you is to get sales rather than kudos then don't necessarily expect press coverage to be the key driver in your sales. Part of my own experience of working with small businesses is that I have seen first-hand that getting national print coverage is great for being able to put a masthead on your website, attracting investment and building your kudos but it doesn't necessarily translate into the big shot in the arm of sales that many brands are expecting.

When I launched Scamp & Dude, we were featured in magazines such as *Vogue* and *Sunday Times Style* but didn't see a large uplift in sales from the coverage. It was the influencer campaigns that really saw a significant spike in sales. It isn't all about sales though, the credibility and awareness gained from print coverage can't be underestimated and I still see print media as an important tool for brands as long as it is teamed with a strong and strategic social media campaign.

ACTIVITY

From section 3.1, you should hopefully now have a bank of tear sheets of product pages. If you don't, go to your newsagent, research online and pull together a list of people you want to pitch to.

In your subject line, make it clear you are pitching for that magazine and have read it by writing a bespoke subject line; e.g., "Pitch for *Stylist*: Style Pick" (Don't use block capitals, it's an absolute *no! no!*).

Craft a personalised email. We all like the feeling when someone has taken the time to write something tailored to us. Start up top with a succinct pitch that matches how they write about a product; e.g., small headline, descriptive one-liner on the product, price and URL. Include a low-res image in the body of your email so they can see what it looks like.

Create a link to your press kit that should include hi-res images. If in any doubt, your image should be 300 dpi and large enough to fill the dimensions of the page.

'About' blurb: after you have written your bespoke pitch in the style of that magazine include any additional information such as a press release, media alert or 'about us'-type product information. I often cut and paste just the boiler plate after the key product information.

PDFs are not your friend

We mentioned PDFs earlier but just as a reminder, journalists are *superbly* busy, mainly due to the major cuts happening in media organisations, so your job is to make their job as easy as possible. You might be able to edit a PDF easily, but this doesn't mean that they can. So, trust me when I say just cut and paste your information into the body of an email.

Don't be afraid of naming your competitors

Again, two is coincidence, three is a trend. Naming other businesses in your category can be a great way to pitch your product as part of a new trend. We did this with The Marshmallowist's CBD mallows and often saw some of our suggestions make the final cut.

The key thing when pitching your product is to keep it simple and succinct and to ensure that you have relevant stockists for the publication. If you have a luxury product, it's not going to work for a title that covers inexpensive brands. Start with key information at the top and if you must add more background, keep it below your initial pitch for further reading so they have it if they want it.

Click on our pitching PDF template for a framework of how to pitch to journalists, including an example we have used, at www.thewern.com/book.

EXAMPLE

When you study enough product pages, you notice that they will all follow a theme. And often you will see similar themes across multiple publications. The 2019 Pantone colour of the year is living coral – cue multiple fashion, interior and product pages in living coral colours. Before that we had yellow, and before that millennial pink. Colour trends can provide a great platform for you to tap into.

I've consulted on and off for The Marshmallowist, who in 2018 relaunched with a brand-new design, and as well as the best sellers, created some quirky new flavours. The range of flavours and the fact that they were combined with booze gave us several different angles to carve up when pitching to product pages. The limited-edition CBD (cannabidiol) mallows proved that PR can be a marathon not a sprint. When the limited box launched, we used the angle of the trend of CBD food products to pitch to media, but in truth in May 2018, there were only a few examples to hand that I could find. By December 2018 there had been a proliferation of new food and drinks brands emerging using CBD and the *Daily Mail* picked up the story (having previously expressed interest in May but put the story on hold). The *Daily Mail* catapulted the CBD product into the mainstream and before we knew it *This Morning* were contacting us (having previously been sent two samples to no avail). It was all about timing – next thing we knew, Phil and Holly couldn't get enough of the sample and the sales went up by 500% compared to the same period in the previous year.

When *This Morning* and the *Daily Mail* expressed interest but didn't immediately pounce on the story, I didn't harass them, send multiple emails or phone them and sometimes sitting tight and knowing that your pitch is a good one takes courage, but it can pay off.

In bigger PR agencies, I've seen product samples sent out willy nilly and to be honest, I do think this can be a waste of money. Ideally, you do want to have product samples to send out, but maybe consider how many you want to issue and to whom. Also, note that gifting does not always equate to coverage.

Lastly, think about where you can place your product that you wouldn't expect. I always think the press coverage that Soda Says gets is amazing because it's not in the usual tech pool you would expect and I asked co-founder Grace Gould a bit more about this:

[A] curated marketplace isn't anything new. Farfetch really pioneered the idea of a curated marketplace and our model is very similar to them. It's just the customer and media are used to having tech really focused in a highly 'gadgety' space. So tech previously has been focused in publications like *PCMag* and *Wired*. We love these publications, but it's also really fun for us to be featured in the fashion and lifestyle pages which isn't where you'd normally see tech products. Lisa Armstrong, the Fashion Editor of *The Telegraph* has been amazing to us covering our products and newsletter very early on in our journey. Likewise, in the US it's the fashion and lifestyle press which our brand has done best in.

TIPS

- Keep it simple and succinct and ensure you have the stockist information and price.
- Do *not* start off your email with "I'm excited to tell you about my brand-new product" – journalists read hundreds of emails a day, many with the *exact* same sentence.

- Try to pitch your product before it launches, many publications only want products that have launched in the last few months.
- If your product has been out for a while, can you put a fresh spin on it; e.g., limited-edition packaging, brand collaboration or linking to a charity?
- Is your product the perfect gift for Christmas, Easter, Mother's Day, etc.?
- Double- and then triple-check that your product is the right fit for that publication.

CHECKLIST

- Is your product 100% relevant to the title you are pitching for?
- Have you included a small image (low-res) inside your email pitch?
- Have you included a link to download the hi-res images?
- What is the name of the column or page you are pitching for?
- If the title you are pitching for is a monthly magazine, have you allowed enough time (usually at least 3 but usually 6 months)?
- Is the price, business URL and stockist information clear and up to date?
- Do you have an allocation of product that you could send to media if they request a sample?

3.4 Guest posts

One of the common questions I get from service-led businesses is how do I get publicity? Particularly, a lot of service-led design, tech, marketing or innovation agencies are not always allowed to talk about the work they have. (*Or* maybe they don't even want to?)

For me, one of the most useful tools for any entrepreneur or service business owner is the much-underrated guest post. For me, this tactic could almost warrant its own book because there are multiple ways to position yourself as an expert to secure guest coverage. Whether you are part of a bigger company or a sole trader, Hyping Yourself in this way is in my opinion the strongest thing you can do.

ACTIVITY

Here is how I structure my pitch emails, which has secured coverage in titles such as Huffington Post, *FT* Opinion, *gal-dem*, *Red* online, *Courier* and *ShortList* (RIP).

Read other guest posts and guidelines

I know, I know. I never just let you get on with the fun stuff, I make you prep first, but seriously, heed my advice. Spend a good hour reading other posts and often the site will have guidelines on how to pitch; e.g., they might want actionable tips, or it might have to be related to the news or they might want a strong crisis over adversity real-life story. Know your title before you pitch. I usually start off with a wish list of the Top Three dream pieces I'd love to get (usually a nationwide.com publication) and maybe three smaller titles that might be easier/quicker to get the ball rolling (such as industry blog or trade publications).

Warning: as an aside, don't write the article first and then look to place it. This is backwards and it means you will not have written in the style for that publication but your own signature style. And one size fits no one, my friend.

Subject line

I always write "Pitch for: Name of column, name of publication and a short headline".

This demonstrates to the journalist immediately that the pitch is tailored to them, you have read the publication and you have crafted something bespoke for them. The headline should be your top pick of an article for them that would grab their readers' attention.

(NB: More on how to find the right journalist in section 3.4.)

Intro

Keep it friendly (not over-friendly) and to the point. Don't bother with the "How are you today?" – journalists are busy, and you probably don't know them so just cut to the chase.

Hello (name – spelt correctly),

My name is XX and I'm an expert in YY and ZZ. Would you be interested in the following ideas for a guest post:

Article ideas

I tend to suggest two or three ideas; it gives the journalist some brain food and the opportunity to give feedback and editorial direction. In an ideal world you are not pitching what they have just covered, but they might already be featuring one of your topics in the pipeline so having a few improves your chances.

I write one sentence per topic with a maximum of 2/3 pithy bullet points underneath.

Examples of previous writing

If you have not had a guest post before that's fine. But use links to a blog on your website, LinkedIn or Medium to demonstrate your writing style. Again, I tend to bullet point a few examples.

Demonstrate wider expertise

Lastly, if relevant, I will include a boiler plate, business bio or personal bio right at the bottom. This provides a wider context and credentials to cement why you might be good for them.

Sign-off

Make sure you have a signature with your email and phone number included. Your email may very well get forwarded on and you want to make sure you are easy to reach.

EXAMPLE

Below is a case study of the exact pitch I used for Davinia Tomlinson, founder of Rainchq, that we used to get into Huffington Post. The article evolved from this initial pitch with suggestions from the opinion editor, but this was the pitch we used to get us through the door and get the ball rolling.

Hi XX,

I'm working with Davinia, one of 12 women who has won a place in part of a tech accelerator programme run out of the Olympic Park and is the founder of Rainchq, a new concept in financial services that targets women that launches on Monday.

To give you context as to why her new service, Rainchq, is needed. The average 65-year-old woman retires on £35,800 — the average man retires with a pension 5 x greater. www. insuringwomensfutures.co.uk/.

In response to recent news [I included two news articles of relevance], I thought it could be timely to draft a guest post along the following lines:

— Opinion piece as to why it is important for all women to learn how to invest
— Why technology is the answer to empower all women regionally, not just a Londoncentric business to invest their money
— How the current financial advice is not even reaching women
— It is important for all women, all backgrounds, all cultures but mostly those who are underrepresented to be given a forum to manage their finances.

Do let me know if this might be of interest.

Thanks

Lucy

As Davinia had just launched Rainchq, we included the press release with a boiler plate and a short bio of herself underneath.

TIPS

- Guest posts shouldn't read like an advertisement for your business. There is nothing more inauthentic then someone banging on about how great their offering is. People want to know about your business challenges, interesting points of view, human interest stories, not a first-hand account from a business owner on why they are great.
- There are countless people who advocate writing guest posts who are also not publicists with a black book; if you don't believe me, ask Susie Moore or Janet Murray.
- It's always great to come up with a long list of topics you can talk about but stick to just three ideas when pitching to a publication.
- Have you got an example of previous writing you can use to demonstrate? If not, post an article on your own blog, LinkedIn and/or Medium.

CHECKLIST

- Write down a list of three dream titles you would love to be featured in and three smaller blogs/ industry titles that might be easier and study them.
- Make sure your subject line is tailored for that publication.
- Have you spelt the journalist's name right?
- Do your article suggestions fit the format of that publication?

- Have you demonstrated your writing ability from previous guest posts/or blog posts on LinkedIn/ Medium?
- Have you included your email and contact number?

Download our free guest post pitching PDF from www. thewern.com/book.

3.5 Podcasts

Podcasts are a great way to Hype Yourself to a niche audience and they are unaffected by social media algorithms. You don't need to be speaking on an iTunes Top 10 to make a dent. There are hundreds of niche podcasts out there. I also recommend podcasts as a great medium for people who might feel a bit more introverted about hyping themselves as they usually take place one-on-one or even from your own phone so you can feel very relaxed.

ACTIVITY

Research

Yeah, yeah, I know I'm making you do more research and homework again but if I can drill *one* idea into your head, it is that one size fits no one and sending a relevant pitch is *the* best thing you can do. If you didn't have a list of podcasts in your target media list, now go through and find some podcasts in your area. Fine to pick some from the iTunes Top 10 but appreciate that these probably receive hundreds of pitches so please try and grab a mix.

Listen

Yes. Egg-sucking. But how do you know you fit for a show if you don't ever listen to them? But genuinely listen, don't just try and cheat like, "I loved your interview with Lucy Werner" – try something more genuine like, "I loved your interview with Lucy Werner and I've already heeded some of her advice when it comes to writing my LinkedIn posts".

Bespoke pitch

Revisit the guest post pitch template in section 3.4 and revisit it for podcasts. Also add to this what you are going to be able to add for the audience of that podcast. Think less about what you want from the podcast interview and more about what you can give.

Size doesn't matter

Remember, we are in the world of small businesses, independent brands and entrepreneurs. Nobody expects you to have 100,000 people on your email list, but it is a good idea to talk about how you will share the experience across your own social channels, who your audience is and your engagement numbers.

Previous examples

I always love a few previous examples of writing to show that my client can deliver. Even if that is a link to a blog post on their own website, LinkedIn or Medium.

Make other people's lives easier

Remember I got you to do your bio and get some decent headshots in Chapter 2? Well either link to these in your pitch *or* to step up your professionalism points have them ready to download from your website. Nothing screams, "I'm totally ready to be booked as a guest" than having all your assets ready. And as someone who pitches a *lot* of people for podcasts, blogposts and guest panels, trust me when I say it is a pain getting images and bios.

EXAMPLES

Going back to all the content you created in the Chapter 1 and Chapter 2 activities you should have a list of areas you can speak about. Mine is very much broken up into the following categories and I would tailor my pitch to different podcasts accordingly.

Female founder

- Women and business books – Why more women should write business books;
  e.g., there are no PR business books in the Top 10 in Amazon but the PRCA says the PR industry is made up of 66% females.
- Why being emotional isn't a bad thing.

Parents in Biz

- Shared parental leave – how shared parental leave allowed me to keep my business going.
- Why my partner's redundancy created a new business opportunity.
- How becoming a parent made my business more profitable and focused.

Small business/Entrepreneur

- PR tips for small businesses (dos and don'ts).
- Lessons I've learnt in business.
- Why 'lifestyle' businesses shouldn't be a dirty word.

TIPS

- Listen to a few different episodes of what you would like to pitch for.
- Reference any shows/interviews that particularly moved you.

- Have you written a compelling subject header on your email?
- Show the synergy between your two audiences; e.g., how you can help or what is interesting about your story.
- Have you considered launching your own podcast? You don't have to do it weekly, you could just do a series.
- Running your own podcast means you could have a legitimate reason to expand your network and approach people that you admire to be guests.

CHECKLIST

- Have you listened to the show? Repeat. Have you *actually* listened to the show?
- Have you spelt the name of the host correctly?
- Have you included some worthy benefits – what their audience will get from you as a speaker?

3.6 Guest panellist

Speaking at local, national and international events can be great for your kudos, building brand awareness, creating connections and driving new business.

Corporate events used to be a bit dry, with a canapé selection not dissimilar to mud on sandpaper and a prerequisite of grey/pinstripe uniform. These days the UK is abuzz with networking and business events to help you learn and grow. What comes with that is increased demand for interesting speakers and events. Speaking at one event well can snowball and lead to all kinds of exposure.

ACTIVITY

- *Does the conference accept guest panels?* If you dig around on most websites, you will find that most have very clear guidelines for guest panellists or at least an events contact/submission form to be a speaker. At this point, you need to make sure you are adhering to their pitching process.
- *Sign up for conference details.* Most of the bigger conferences will issue a call for speakers, some of the bigger ones might invite you to pitch over a portal. Google 'call for speakers', particularly within the fields you are interested in.
- *Practise, practise and practise.* Nobody minds a bit of a jittery speaker if the content is good but a robot (Hi there Maybot) gets boring. Consider investing in some public speaking training.
- *Start small.* Consider events that might be more skill sharing for free in your local community at the beginning. It might not be the sort of thing that raises your profile but is good for your soul. It's also great practice to get on stage, hold a mic and polish your delivery.

  It is particularly good if you can get a video footage of you speaking, even if it is a quick recording via Facebook Live at an event that you can use to issue to demonstrate your experience. But do also create a list of dream events that you would love to speak at that are way above your day-to-day usual aspirations. Really aim high on this one and don't let your self-limiting beliefs get in the way.

— *Join some networking groups/attend events.* In January this year I decided to join a few different networking groups and to attend as many events as possible. By exploring all the different event opportunities out there and the possibilities that are out there, I felt it gave me a real idea of what worked well and what I thought could be improved on. From seeing various presentations, it also gave me an idea of the type of content I would like to prepare.

— *Bigger conferences work far in advance.* Within 1–2 months of a large international event finishing, they will start to open up registration for the next one and for submission for speakers and it is worth registering for these for the reminder.

EXAMPLE

Cannes Lions – Aim high without fear

When I pitched for Cannes Lions International Festival of Creativity, the world's biggest creative festival, I submitted speaker submissions from five businesses, but it wasn't the CEO with big global clients and high turnovers that was successful. It was female founder Samantha Clarke, owner of the Growth & Happiness School who secured a speaker pass for a happiness workshop.

It was at this moment that I realised that even I, a PR professional for the best part of 15 years, can have self-limiting beliefs. With Sam, I just punted it and hoped for the best. It was beyond my wildest dreams that we secured an actual spot for her. It taught me a huge lesson that often when it comes to print coverage, we all aim for nationals or bigger titles, but when it comes to speaking slots, we tend to start low. My recommendation is 100% build your strategy at the lower tiers, but don't be afraid of shooting for a few global stages because you just never know.

We pitched in September and had our slot confirmed by February. As well as the kudos of being a speaker, the event was an invaluable platform for networking.

TIPS

We spoke with Kate Mander, Senior Talent Producer for The Stylist Group who is responsible for sourcing talent for *Stylist* Live, as well as other *Stylist* events and for commercial content to get her 10 top tips for getting on the radar of people who book events.

1. *Email pitches:* I welcome email pitches of new talent to introduce themselves. Keep them concise:
   - Who are you and what are your credentials?
   - How would you like to collaborate?
   - Associated links i.e. your website, showreel

2. *Examples:* I love it when people provide videos and practical examples of their work; it can be a risk punting on someone you don't know, so anecdotal evidence of them in practice means that I can see them in action and build a better picture of how they could work for our audience.

3. *Preparation:* Do your research – make sure you understand the audience and what we are about. For example, pitching a weight loss talk is never going to work for us as it's not something we would ever feature on our platforms. Come with ideas of how you can inspire our audience. We want to provoke conversation not follow it, so what topical things do you have to say? How are you going to help move the conversation on in your area?

4. *Takeaways:* As part of your workshop/talk ideas, what four things will our audience learn/what are the takeaways from the session? Our audience are hungry for facts and practical tips which they will be able to practically implement into their lives. We are focused on not being preachy but inspiring our audience, so demonstrating how you can do this is key.

5. *Invitations:* If you are launching a new product, speaking at an event or you have a book out for example, then invite me along. We work on multiple content all year round and are

always looking for new exciting talent to work with. It might be that this email comes in at the right time and you are just what we are looking for and is a legitimate reason to be in touch.

6. *Instagram:* Connect with me on Instagram, I'm not a huge poster, but again if you are on my radar, it could be I find just the right thing at the right time.

7. *Contact/context:* 100% send me a short bio at the end of your pitch, a contact number, link to your handles and website, but no CVs. I'm after a bespoke pitch, not to hire you.

8. *Tone:* Confidence not cocky – avoid "I'm perfect, why haven't you booked me yet?". I 100% want to see confidence and I want people to reach out but get the balance right.

9. *Hype yourself:* Just like the title of this book suggests, being talent right now is very exciting and there are so many opportunities to put yourself out there. And by talent, I don't mean just celebrities, I mean being an expert, having an inspiring career, having a triumph over adversity story.

10. *Time it right: Stylist* Live happens in November and I am inundated with pitches in the week after that event for the following year. But that is far too soon, we start discussing our content about 6 months before the event so that's the time to make contact.

3.7 Write for the national news

One of the most undervalued PR opportunities across the board is the letter, comment and opinion pages of national news and magazines. If getting into a national newspaper is your goal, this should be the *first* place you look to, particularly if writing is your strength.

Not only that, but *new* writers, new talent, new thinking is always of interest to opinion editors. In the last year alone, I've seen some fantastic contributions from people who are small business owners, freelancers or just experts in their own field who don't need to have a million-pound turnover business behind them to get their views across.

So, what is the difference between letters, comment and opinion?

Letters to the editor

A letter is usually short, with a quick turnaround, and might support, argue or build on a news story that has already been covered. Unlike a comment or opinion piece, I would *always* submit a letter in full and keep it in the exact style in which it has been written. Most daily newspapers publish in the region of at *least* five letters a day. Ideally, to be in the best chance of publication I would be looking to get your letter in response drafted and submitted by 10 am on the *same day* of publication. The PR expert in me is trained that to be successful you *have* to be able to respond quickly. If you submit a letter in response at 4:30 pm you are too late for the next day's paper. And the reality is, you have missed the news window.

Comment/Opinion pieces

This is a longer-form piece of content. Not dissimilar to the idea of writing a guest post or a blog post. Only papers are not looking for top tip articles or your takeaways. They are looking for strong, pithy articles that can cause debate. Remember, at the end of the day it is *all* about clicks. So, the more divisive an article, the better it is for the paper because if people start to engage online or on socials it gives them wider exposure = bigger readership = ability to command bigger advertising fees from brands = newspaper being more profitable. Unlike the letter, I would *not* draft this in full *but* provide an outline of what this could look like.

ACTIVITY

- Yup, you guessed it. *Read.* Whether you are pitching for Indy Voices or the *FT* Letters' page. There are very distinct editorial tones of voice and styles for each. So, revisit your target media list from Chapter 1 and study these columns.
- If you know there is a particular slot you want to go for, then read on a regular basis so you

become an expert in who contributes and the style that they print.

- Do not be put off if you are different from the usual contributor. I have regularly seen call outs for more women, more BAME, more youth contributors because let's face it, the era of a man in a suit with decades of business experience being the barometer for success is over. The number of SMEs has grown phenomenally in the last decade and with that we need contributors to reflect this new disparity in the working world.

- SME owners are in *the* best place to turn content around quickly, so once you see an article or story you want to comment on you need to pounce and *quickly*. So, make sure you have the basics of your pitch sandwich created. The top and tail is your intro, examples of writing and bio. Have a skeletal email written out (don't forget your contact details) and then make sure you write a tailored pitch to *that* publication in response to their story.

- Make sure you read and re-read the editorial guidelines for the publication you are writing for.

EXAMPLE

This would be subject to change depending on the editorial guidelines, but this is an example opinion pitch that I would construct.

Dear XX

Following the news of XX or this article (insert example article you are responding to – ideally from the same publication), I would like to offer a counter opinion on the following:

Synopsis: Insert the headline of your opinion piece here

3–5 sentences on the crux of your argument

About 'insert your name'

Include a small biography of yourself here to demonstrate why you are well placed to comment on this.

Examples of writing:

Include 2/3 links of opinion pieces you have already done, if possible.

Thanks

Sign off with your name

TIPS

We spoke with Jess Austin, opinion editor of the *Metro* on some best practice tips for pitching an opinion piece:

- Timing
  If you think your client is the perfect person to write [a] comment piece on the back of a news story, pitch the idea as soon as possible. Most papers will want a same day turnaround so [as] to make sure you'll be able to get it to the editor in good time.
- Need a slower turnaround time?
  Then don't pitch into reaction to the news agenda and [instead] look at what series the site is running. It's a good way to get someone's voice published without them having to commit to a same day turnaround and if it's not linked to a news story it's a better opportunity for them to share their story or brand.
- Issuing a report?
  If you've got a report out, send an embargoed copy around as soon as you can before it goes live. There may be something in it that could form the basis of an opinion piece or news story. Even better, send some suggestions of opinion pieces you can write with it.
- Pitch format
  In order of priority, this is what I am looking for from a well written pitch email:
  - What is the news story you are pitching on the back of?

- What is the angle your client would want to take?
- Who are they and what is their experience? Why are they the best person to write it?
- What are the points they would make?
- How soon can they write it?

- Big No, Nos
  Never pitch asking a journalist 'broadly, what are you looking for?' The answer is always on the website. Look at what they've published recently and let that be your guide.

CHECKLIST

- Have you checked the publication's guidelines and what they have previously published to make sure that what you are pitching is relevant?
- Can you actually turn around the content for your idea quickly? The last thing you want is a green light to say, yes, we want you to write this and then for you to never deliver.
- Is your opinion different/surprising?
- Are you prepared for people to disagree/not like your opinion?

3.8 Hosting your own event

Many people think that they *need* to host an event to get their company name out there, launch a product or celebrate a milestone. If budgets are tight, I would say that this really isn't the case as they can all too often be vanity projects. That said, executed well, a pop-up of a bricks & mortar space for an online or service business can be a huge awareness booster.

If you don't already have a huge following or engaged audience, then selling tickets to events can be one of the biggest struggles I see businesses face. The biggest piece of advice I can give on this is to make sure you are giving yourself plenty of time to try out different tactics to build your follower base.

The other thing to consider is who you are selling your tickets with. Many ticket sales sites such as Eventbrite or Billetto will work with you to promote your event. Speak to them to see if there are any opportunities to collaborate; e.g., are they doing a blog post or newsletter to their audience with guest content that you could contribute to? Equally, pop-up hubs like Appear Here will often offer PR and marketing support to run alongside your pop-up experience so it is always worth enquiring with your event partner, whoever that may be, on how you can amplify and hype your event.

ACTIVITY

Before your event – consider the following activity:

- Does this make the best use of my budget *or* would I get a better return on investment from spending on a different activity?

- If your budget is tight, could you find an event sponsor or a brand partner to reduce costs?
- What is the objective of your event?
- Does your event objective meet one of your business activities?

Write an event or listings release

The reason it can be called 'listings' is because the section that a lot of events are featured in are called listings. Otherwise known as: to-do guides, diary pages, what's on guides, what do this weekend:

- Make sure you have the five Ws answers up top: who, what, when, where and why.
- Can you include a reason as to *why* it is relevant now or can you highlight a trend?
- What is interesting about your event? Make it really clear and spell it out up top.
- Are you doing a promotion that will add value to readers; e.g., first 100 people will get a free XX, anyone with a certain name gets it free, 50% off for first three days?

Compile a media list of all the publications that you would like to feature your event

I would do what I call the 'tear sheet' exercise here. Where you go through *where* you want your event featured and rip out all the columns it can work for. Don't forget about all the online sites and newsletters you might like to be featured in. So, if for example, you want to be included in LeCool London, then make sure you are subscribed and reading on a regular basis, so you know the names of the slots.

Create a spreadsheet of the slots

There is more detail about compiling a media list in section 3.1. But I would make sure ahead of schedule you are creating a list of all the target columns you want to be in. Don't forget about influencers and video content too. For example, securing video content for *Time Out* or *Cosmopolitan* for your pop-up with the video team can significantly boost your awareness and reach.

Create your timeline

If you want to be in *Time Out* print, you need to be going out to listings or newswires at *least* six weeks in advance. If you want to be included in the diary pages of monthly magazines, you need to be pitching 3–6 *months* in advance. So, depending on your slots make sure you are sending out your information in plenty of time. In some instances, they may do a last minute compile 10-days or a week before but it is far better to be too early than too late.

Images

I always include a low-res image within my email pitch to media and a link to download high-res. If you want to secure a prominent slot in a publication you need a good event image. Obviously, if this hasn't happened yet, it can be hard to capture so you need to think of how you can illustrate the event.

EXAMPLE

The first time we worked with Blondies Kitchen, other than the fact they had a *brilliant* product and the founders had a *fab* story, we secured them three mentions across different sections of *Time Out* amongst the raft of media coverage to launch them.

- We talked about a new trend and how it already existed in the US and was now coming over here which means it didn't just work for listing but had a trend angle too.
- We don't try and cram all the information up top, you discover more information when you keep reading.
- The full menu and prices are at the end in Editors' Notes, but the key info (the five Ws) are right up top.
- They had images of themselves with and without the cookies, so we had additional assets we needed for media.
- We invited media down to come and try the cookies.

TIPS

For a long time, when I was hosting lifestyle events in London, the Holy Grail for me was to be featured on LondOntheinside. I asked co-founder Jules Pearson for some top tips to help you think about how to hype your event:

- The title of the event in the subject line will make me open your email if the event is interesting enough. Sum it up in a few sentences and include a few photographs but only to add value and demonstrate the event (no stock shots).
- Don't worry about branded gifts. I don't need another USB chargeable branded mini speaker thanks.
- Don't create a stunt or event that is irrelevant to your brand or business, especially if jumping on the bandwagon and already overdone. Try to create something more authentic to the brand which is either topical or based on whatever the trends might be at that time/on the horizon. Topical events always work well because people relate to the content at that point in time, actively looking for activations based around days.
- In the last five years there has been an explosion of events and some have been down right silly – so silly that they have been cancelled due to ethical reasons or consumer

complaints. Instagram has influenced the explosion and we've seen events/pop-ups created solely for the purpose of Instagram – the ice-cream museum and pizza museum are great examples and whilst these might look great on people's feeds in real-life, they tend to be a bit depressing with long queues, one Instagram moment, expensive ticket prices and that's about it. Eventually people will get wise to this and the Instagram bubble will burst (one can only hope!).

CHECKLIST

- Have you got the day of the week, date, venue and time spelt correctly right up the top?
- Do you have some portrait/landscape imagery (decent imagery) that can be used to illustrate the event?
- Is there an opportunity to invite local media?
- Have you Googled 'submit an event listing for XX' (for XX insert region of where you live)? A quick search will pull up a whole bunch of places where you can list your event online for free.

3.9 Feature pitch tips

We discussed how to craft a feature pitch in Chapter 2.6 but in this section, I want to talk about how you take those ideas and how to pitch them. The lead-time for pitching to a news desk is very quick, but with a feature writer you often have more space to take your time and can plan in advance. For example, you might have identified a great new consumer behaviour trend but need to wait for the right newshook to peg it onto.

Rather than aiming straight for a national newspaper, consider pitching a feature angle to your local news, niche trade title or an online publication first and work your way up to the big guns.

It's also important not to forget the importance of branded content. There are more opportunities than ever before to be featured by brands' own publications. I would encourage you all to engage with this new media wave; e.g., the high readership of NatWest ContentLive makes it just as credible and useful for your business as a national neswspaper's online business section.

Reminder: features are long-form trend articles that often mention several examples of case studies or businesses. They are not always labelled as features on websites or in magazines so you will need to do your research to identify what they look like.

ACTIVITY

- Go back to the feature topics you have pulled out and make sure you have a calendar date or relevant newshook from the content you created in Chapter 1.6.

- If you don't have a reason to go 'right now' consider holding onto your pitch until a suitable newshook becomes available.
- Check the features for the media outlet (or whatever they are labelled as) and read through their current format.
- Are you providing assets; e.g., not just an idea but what you can support your trend with?
  - ○ Can you offer case studies?
  - ○ Quotes from industry experts?
  - ○ Do you have any strong photography of infographic data visuals that could accompany the piece?
  - ○ Are you ensuring that you are telling the story of a wider industry piece rather than just an article based on yourself?
- Identify the name of the features journalist who is writing about your topic/area. If the name is not obvious, can you find the name of the commissioning editor or features director?
- Write a clear subject line (not in capslock) explaining the angle; e.g., "Pitch for National Pet Week – Pets make workers more productive".
- Ensure you give the journalist enough time to give feedback. Pick *one* journalist to pitch your feature to and tailor it to them. A polite chase once or twice to see if it's relevant is fine but give them some time. If you don't hear back this is likely to be a no, so allow yourself enough time to take the feature to a few different publications *or* pitch out to a few different freelance feature writers who you have identified as fitting your list.

EXAMPLE

I've pitched a *lot* of features in my time, but the example I want to share with you is back from my agency days to help demonstrate how as a company you can think outside the box. One of my favourite things about PR is taking people and businesses outside the pages where you might expect to see them.

In this example, I was working for a digital company, The BIO Agency. They have a brilliant company culture epitomised by the founder Peter Veash's office dog Phillip. I looked in national days coming up and identified it was National Pet Week. We then put out a few questions via Censuswide as a research story around levels of creativity and pets in the workplace. They helped source a list of case studies of unusual pets in offices. I took the package of:

- Research stats including Top 10 unusual animals as well as trend-led stats on pets boosting office creativity
- Case studies of unusual office pets
- Quotes from CEOs/office workers on why they love their office pet

and I went to a national freelancer, Hazel Davis, who at that time was writing a lot about creative businesses and office culture. I then helped source additional assets and she secured the piece on the front page of the now defunct *Guardian Work* supplement and a full three-page spread. As I pitched it to her far in advance of National Pet Week, she also had time to pitch it to an editor and secure her own commission.

TIPS

- Make sure you are providing at least three examples. Just using your own business isn't enough.
- Check the big four: Deloitte, PwC, Ernst & Young and KPMG are well respected for reports and research. Consider using some stats from their recent research to provide a topical newshook.
- A great idea is always better than how well it is written. A weak story cannot be made into a good story, but a bit of bad punctuation won't ruin a compelling story. So, make sure you start with a strong idea.

3.10 News desks

A common myth I experience with strangers to publicity is this notion that they have created something newsworthy just by creating a new business and writing a press release about it.

Stories I warn against issuing as news:

- New branding or website
- New hire (unless you are the CEO of Apple, for example)
- Award wins
- New product launch
- New company launches.

You may think the above is contradictory to what I am saying throughout the book, so I want to be really clear. I would not issue this to news desk writers. Instead below, I've put examples of where this might be issued:

- *New branding or website:* If the design is phenomenal *maybe* this might be of interest to creative titles as a case study with the results of how the rebrand has completely changed the sales for your business. Otherwise, this is just for your media kit/website.
- *New hire* (unless you are the CEO of Apple, for example): This can be a great way to make contact with media as an FYI, but I would select maybe the business desk or feature writers of your vertical titles and off the back of the new hire, pitch some guest posts for the person appointed.
- *Award wins:* Great as an FYI for your local publications but again, use as an opportunity to pitch for a bigger business profile or interview.
- *New product launch:* There are specific writers who cover product roundups or you may pitch the press release with a bespoke note to trend writers.
- *New company launch:* There are millions of SMEs, this is not 'news', *but* within your own vertical trade (e.g., food – *The Grocer* or fashion – *Drapers*), there might be specific columns or areas, or pitch news related to your business.

Nadine Sandcroft from JustEntrepreneurs.co.uk comments:

> It is really obvious who has taken the time to research the site versus those who just issue the press release far and wide and hope we will cover as news. The press releases that I pay attention to are those that are issued with a bespoke pitch with a considered email of where the story might fit or could be part of our website.

EXAMPLE

One of my favourite viral news stories I've worked on in recent years was a story for Hari Ghotra: the Indian chef was launching her first curry kits and had created a UK map that revealed, surprisingly, that Southerners liked it hotter.

What assets did you use?

Her own inhouse design team created a UK heat map with a clear key that showed the parts of the UK that liked it hotter, with clear dark/hotter patches in the South than the North; this was issued with a press release that broke down the research.

How did you sell this in?

We had a pre-created media list of:

- All national news desks – these are generic email addresses that can be found on the national newspaper websites and typically don't change.
- We also phoned switchboards at 08:30 am on launch day and asked to be put forward to the news desk and verbally pitch in the story. If of interest, they might send us an individual address, but if not, we moved on.
- Pitch on phone is succinct, news desks are busy, so we went straight in with "Hello, are you interested in a research story from an Indian chef with a heat map that shows, surprisingly, that Southerners like it hotter than Northerners?"
- We would follow up with a tailored email to each contact and the press release cut and pasted underneath.
- The heat map and all other associated imagery was attached.
- We also issued it to any food journalists who from our desk research had covered quirky news before as well as the food trade.
- We also picked off a couple of key regions – Birmingham, as this is where Hari is from; and Surrey, as this is where she lives now.

Why the story worked

- Brits love their curry and it is seen as a very quintessentially British thing; the story was focused on the UK as a nation, so it tapped into the national news agenda.

- It was fun, quirky and surprising – we all know the stereotypes that Southerners are soft, and Northerners are harder. So, the story was going against the grain and showing a new trend.
- We had ready-made assets, which meant the whole story was already written for the media, the illustrated heat map was used by almost everyone who covered the story which goes to show, if done correctly, infographics are fab assets to use.
- A heat map typically refers to actual temperature heat, so the fact it related to the intensity of curry flavour gave it additional comic spin.

Examples of why a news story doesn't work

Yes of course I have examples. This doesn't mean that I'm rubbish, it means that sometimes things happen that are outside of my control and I'm constantly learning:

- An influx of breaking news can dominate all the news slots and so there isn't physical space to get a look in.
- Loads of PRs are pitching news stories at once and papers will only allocate a certain percentage to funny/bizarre stories and on the day, they had a better story.
- Over-complicating the story – a big watch out particularly if you are doing data or research is to try and sell too many stories. You want 3/4 stats max that back up one trend or data point. Further down you can maybe add more data points, but with too many the actual story can get lost.

- Your pitch isn't tight enough – when you are working so close to something you need an external point of view to check it over to remind you that it's too complicated and to simplify it.
- No genuine newshook – in a crowded and cluttered news market why does your story matter now?

TIPS

These are the questions you should ask yourself before contacting any news desk:

- Would this interest their readers; e.g., if you are going to the *FT*, think of the business readership.
- Why is this story relevant today? What is the newshook?
- What is so different/unusual about this story?
- Do you have any evidence to back up your claim or trend? The evidence must be recent and substantial – a poll of 21 of your customers won't cut it.
- Unlike junior PRs in agencies who have no choice but to chase journalists because someone senior to them has signed off a news release, you don't *have* to pitch to a news desk. If you are going to phone the lion's den, make sure it is relevant.

Some notes on what not to do:

- Create a news desk media list and send it out on a b'cc to all addresses. This is called spam. And arguably you will fall foul of GDPR (General Data Protection Regulation) guidelines.

– Pitch something that happened the day before, it isn't news anymore, that was the day before.

– Make sure there is a story that isn't focused on the brand. In both the examples above, there was something quirky to see or try rather than the companies' key sales message that gave it traction.

CHECKLIST

– Check Sky News before you even consider picking up the phone; if there is major breaking news going on then forget about it because this is what the nationals are going to be focused on.

– Do you have plenty of assets ready; e.g., a succinct storyline, a spokesperson, imagery if required?

– Is it timely?

3.11 Interviews and Q&As

There are plentiful opportunities for business or personal interviews to help Hype Yourself.

When I started in PR 15 years ago, the only slots available for business were aimed at corporates with a turnover of £2.5 million plus. Today, the blurring of the work/life balance, portfolio careerists and the rise of the side-hustlers means the media landscape has changed and there are plenty of opportunities for Q&As.

Size doesn't matter. Repeat. Size doesn't matter. Leave your ego at the door and start small. Look at which blogs or Instagram feeds feature or interview business founders in your niche.

ACTIVITY

- Check out the peers and competitors of your business and see where they are being featured and use this to build a list of niche slots and columns you can pitch for.
- Keep a notebook to hand when you are on Instagram, or browsing the net and make sure you note down any relevant columns/bloggers you could work with.
- Cross-reference this interview list with your business objectives, target audience and target media list from Chapter 1 to make sure you are keeping on brand.
- Look at service industries in your area – e.g., many marketing, design and PR agencies I know who focus on small businesses also like to profile small businesses. The regular feed of interesting businesses is a great opportunity for them to expand their reach but also for you to be featured.
- Brands in general have some fabulous content: Monzo, NatWest ContentLive, Virgin StartUp or UnderPinned are all examples of businesses playing in the space that I am in where editorial content informs a key part of their strategy.

EXAMPLE

On first glance you might think Davinia from Rainchq, whose business is to empower women to invest, could only be profiled for fintech and trade-specific publications. But after revisiting our business objectives and identifying that we wanted to grow her consumer audience we re-imagined her strategy.

Dav is also a mum, so we started to pitch to parent-led blogs as an opportunity to raise her personal profile and humanise her brand and pitched her to be in the Mum's The Word Events blog. Unless you are in the parent world, it isn't a title you are likely to stumble upon. No shade to the gals but they are engaging and speaking with a particular demographic. And let me tell you something. This Q&A led directly to her business objectives, it helped grow her customer database *and* off the back of this, she was invited by Scummy Mummies, owner of the UK's number one parenting podcast with over 90,000 followers on Instagram to appear on the podcast.

Within the same fortnight, Davinia also appeared in a feature on the Forbes website which is also mega for kudos and SEO. But to give some perspective, the Forbes mention might look more impressive to the outside world, but the Mum's The Word Q&A worked so much harder for her business objectives, driving sales and sign-ups.

EXAMPLE

Subject line: "Founder of fintech service that empowers women to invest for 'Mama Meets' column".

Then in the body of the email I crafted something that is really tailored for that title; e.g.,

> I work with Davinia Tomlinson, founder of Rainchq, a service that empowers women to invest. As well as a fintech juggernaut, she also is the mother of two children, and I thought her start-up story as well as finance tips would be of interest to your readers. Particularly as mothers we struggle more with the gender pay gap and long-term pension poverty.
>
> Thanks
>
> Lucy [making sure my email and phone number are in my signature]

(Underneath, I would also include a biography, and either the business boiler plate or a press release as background information.)

TIPS

- Make sure your ego doesn't block you from pitching for interviews in smaller niche titles.
- Check your competitors or other people in your industry to get ideas of where you could be.

- Think outside the box – I'm a PR but I rarely pitch for PR interview slots, I focus on niches where my audience is.

CHECKLIST

- Have you created a quality over quantity wish list of slots you would like to be in?
- Have you read the various interviews/slots to check you are relevant?
- Can you source the right person to pitch to?
- Have you included your bio and boiler plate in the pitch?

Chapter summary

In this chapter, you should start learning to use the materials you crafted in Chapter 2 but always returning to your blueprint from Chapter 1. By now, I hope you have an understanding of the traditional press office function and how to commence a basic media relations campaign.

We've covered off different journalists – what the different desks do and identifying which journalists you need to build relationships with.

On your media database, we have looked at how to create the backbone of your press office with a media database.

- Products: How and where you should pitch your product.
- Guest posts: How to pitch for a guest article.
- Features: How to pitch to a features desk.
- Podcasts: How to secure a podcast interview.
- Panels: How to pitch to be on a panel.
- Interviews and Q&As: How to secure one.

In Chapter 4, we are going to explore more creative ways to pitch your business, so hold onto your hats.

CHAPTER 4

THE BRAIN FARTS

OK, so to recap you now have a tight PR plan in place and you're armed with the basic tactical media relations to commence your press office. Brain farts are what I call the creative ideas that can pop into your head. They are not necessarily the obvious tactics but can be fantastic ways to create cut-through in a cluttered media landscape where everyone is fighting for spaces to hype themselves.

Going back to the content calendar you created in Chapter 1, have a look at any significant gaps where you need to create some of your own content for PR purposes *or* perhaps you have an event, launch or other opening that provides you with an opportunity to think beyond just writing a news release or creating a post for social media.

Whilst writing this book, I attended a talk by Sam Coniff Allende, author of *Be More Pirate*; I wish I could bottle his brain and pour a shot of his thoughts for everyone who gets this far in the book. Because he reminded me you don't need big budgets to do your own publicity stunts. Great publicity is like a dark art but with a touch of bravado, a simple and engaging story and on a quiet news day you might have the perfect blend to create cut-through and even go viral.

Without further ado let's crack on and get you thinking. We are going to be looking at the following:

- Newsjacking – How you can react to the news agenda to create a simple story
- Picture stories – How you can commission a photographer to tell your story
- Video stories – Similar to picture but what you need to consider when making video news
- Influencers – The multiple ways you can work with them
- Research – How working with a research partner can up your chances for coverage
- TV and Radio – The broadcast opportunities for a small business
- Social media – How I recommend using these channels to hype yourself
- Business book – Why you should consider hyping yourself by writing a book.

4.1 Newsjacking

What if your news is old news or you have nothing exciting to say right now, and you need to find a way to speak to media? I think before the social media era, this was just called "how to be a great reactive publicist", but David Meerman Scott coined this neat word in his book of the same name in 2011.

Newsjacking is what it sounds like: it's when you find some news to jack to create your own story. We typically see some brilliant newsjacking on social media, but this can also be pre-planned if you know there is an occasion coming up.

This is where being an early bird comes into play, you need to respond to media quickly if you have a story to react to. Whilst bigger PR agencies lead the way in demonstrating how to do this, it is actually harder for them than for you because:

- They can't just activate on behalf of the client; they would need to have client sign-off.
- Once the agency has gone through the process of securing sign-off for the client, they also will have internal procedures for sign-off.
- If a journalist wants a quick response or answer they are being filtered by the agency.

ACTIVITY

Which leads me nicely to introducing one of the best newsjackers I know, Sophie Raine, deputy MD of W Communications.

I'd be a rich woman if I had a pound for every time a small business owner said to me "but we don't have the kind of money that (insert bigger brand) does...".

What so often goes unrealised is ultimately cash doesn't equate to creativity and actually some of the most memorable and successful PR campaigns cost very little.

This leads me to point 1 of my top 5 tips for small businesses to adopt bigger agency thinking, and by the way everything below that I'm suggesting could be done for free:

1. Try adopting a CONVERSATION FIRST mindset. Instead of always focussing on the news you want to broadcast about your business, focus on existing conversations happening amongst consumers and within the media. Another great example of this is the quick ad Acne mocked up when designer brand Balenciaga released a £1,670 bag that looked incredibly similar to IKEA's Frakta bag.

2. Mine your business for stories. The first thing I do when inducting a new brand is look at what existing collateral they have that we could build stories from. This can be anything from the people in the business to the innovation coming out of it. A great example of this was a campaign many years ago by Frank PR for Pizza Express. During the onboarding sessions the team at Frank unearthed that there was a man whose sole job was to taste the world's tomatoes from across the globe to select which ones were

fit for inclusion in Pizza Express restaurants. A quick rename of his job title to the 'Tommelier' (because if a sommelier picks the wine, why not a tommelier to pick the tomatoes, get it?) resulted in top-tier global press coverage for Pizza Express. Another great campaign that cost absolutely nothing.

3. Find natural 'moments' across the calendar for your brand. There are plenty of news hooks and talking points throughout the year – from Pride to Pie Week, Veganuary to Valentine's Day, International Women's day to Italian Cuisine Week – you catch my drift. Identify the moments that you could naturally play within. It needn't be complicated either. We had a doughnut client who wanted cut-through during chocolate-dominated Easter. They also had the ability to create new variations quickly with their very talented chef – enter the nation's favourite Easter treats reimagined in doughnut form – from the Creme Egg filling to the Mini Egg crust. Resulting in over 20 pieces of press coverage and a queue out the door for the first batch.

4. Identify your audiences' influences. A friend of mine who owned a local restaurant asked me how he could get his brunch offering into a national newspaper or glossy magazine. Before I committed to the challenge, I wanted to delve into the customers a bit more. A couple of free brunches later and

it was evident that the bulk of customers were yummy mummies. It became obvious quite quickly that as amazing as a piece in *Grazia* would be, the real way to win for the restaurant would be to infiltrate these mums' lives in a much deeper way. I wrote a communications plan entirely focussed on reaching this audience via the places they hang out offline (school gates, local yoga studio) and online (they all cited the hyper local Facebook groups as a key recommendation driver). Within 6 weeks of activating the plan, footfall to the restaurant increased by 46%.

5. Keep your eyes and ears open. I'm going to tell you the secret to what makes a best-in-class PR practitioner. It's having a natural thirst for news, an eye on new trends and the ability to (and enjoyment of) consuming media in all forms. It's then marrying this understanding of the media landscape with a deep understanding of your client's business that will help deliver genuine impact. The good news is, if you're reading this book, you're working within a business or own a business and therefore no one, including the world's leading PR agencies, will know the business as well as you. So, the next step is to make sure you're informed so you can marry the business understanding with complete cultural awareness. Yes, the media landscape is rapidly continuing to evolve, and you're not

alone in finding the latest social networks rather flummoxing, but try to see this as an opportunity – there are more spaces than ever for your business to be talked about. You need to be abreast of what's going on in the world, in your industry/sector, what your competitors are up to and back to my earlier point what those who influence your customers are doing, saying and sharing.

EXAMPLE

The most competitive category every year at the PR industry's most prestigious awards (PRWeek Awards) is the "Best Use of a Small Budget". The 2018 winning campaign actually cost a meagre £225 (Taylor Herring's "Beano Vs Jacob Rees-Mogg").

The great thing about the Beano campaign was it was exceptionally cheap, it generated tons of brand-fitting press coverage and that it all came about because of a conversation that was *already happening* on social media. Adopting this 'conversation first' mentality is something W has been working closely with Unilever on across all of their food brands. In turn, we've managed to create an agile low investment (the average idea cost is just £500), high return PR function for them, which has exponentially increased their talkability across editorial, digital and influencer channels.

TIPS

- Remember that you only have a short window to newsjack, make sure you have time to be reactive so that you can see it all the way through.
- Make sure you have a reason to be in that space and you are not hi-jacking. International Women's Day is a classic to see brands jumping on, many of whom don't have a right to be there.
- If you are struggling for ideas look at the many PR resources such as Campaign Experiential, PRmoment or PR Examples to get a flavour for the sort of stunts that work.
- Don't waste a big budget on a newsjacking stunt. As a small agile business, you are in a place to test out as many of these as you can on a budget.

CHECKLIST

- Compile a list of keywords that are relevant for your business — make sure you set up alerts or are searching these regularly to react to.
- Follow some experts who regularly share PR activations to spark ideas.
- If you spot something that is relevant, make sure you react quickly.
- Not every idea will take off but have you tasked yourself with a number to try?

4.2 Picture stories

Every single publication has a picture editor and is looking for news stories in pictures on a daily basis. And in my PR life I've had a lot of success with pitching a story to the business pages based on a photo alone, so if you have not previously considered it, now is the time to get thinking about how you can use pictures to maximise your story.

I *love* a picture stunt; I work a lot in the UK with TNR, which is part of the Press Association's picture desk, to develop a compelling photo story. Brands can often be put off by the cost of doing these – it usually starts from £750 for a PA photographer, but by working with a picture agency, your image more often than not gets put on the newswires, which means it goes to every picture desk editor across the country. The photographers that they send for your job are also experts in telling stories via photos so will come with their own ideas to help sell your story.

Ideas for when a picture story is good to hype yourself:

- *Celebrities:* Many small businesses and entre-preneurs have friends in high places, inviting them to provide a quote and be part of a photo call for your campaign can be great exposure.
- *A new product launch:* Consistently, I've always thought Royal Mail stamps and Madame Tussauds always do a new product unveil really well. It's the classic artist just finishing up the wax work or someone holding a bigger mock-up of the

stamp that always does really well. You 100% need the product image on a white background as I mentioned in Chapter 2, but can you do this in a bigger way?

- *Are you doing something topical for the season:* e.g., a limited-edition dish on the menu for Easter, a quirky pop-up for Christmas?
- *Have you just received a slug of investment, secured a new stockist, hit a milestone in terms of sales?* Business pages are always looking for quirky images to mark a business story so that on its own with a caption can be enough to get coverage.

ACTIVITY

If you have the budget to pay for your own photography, these are the need-to-know steps to issue a photo story as picture news for national and online media. Please be aware that the timings for national are always faster than your local paper which might only appear weekly.

Identify your picture

Your hero image may change but before you do the shoot, plan out a few different shots you can take on the day and ensure that it tells the story clearly.

Map out your timings

This is the most important part. If it's Monday and you want to be in Tuesday's papers you need to be shooting ideally before 9:00 am on the Monday morning, that way your photographer has time to turn around the edit. And you can send your shortlist off before midday. It is *highly* unlikely that anything issued outside of newswires after 2:00 pm will make the papers the next day. If your shoot is in the afternoon/evening, it is even less likely to make the next day print *but* you can still issue for 'pics of the day' as most nationals have online picture carousels and sometimes the weekend papers do a roundup of the best shots of the week.

Prepare your media list

Ensure you have the details of the picture editor *or* the desk you are pitching to. If you are selling a picture story in for the business desk, for example, then you will need the business reporter. A Google search or phone call to the switchboard should be able to provide you with the generic email address for the desk you need.

Subject line

Ensure your subject line clearly tells the story.

EXAMPLE

The following example is a template that can be used for inviting media for a photo or video call, although obviously the filming/photography options differ between the two. You can, however, use this template tweaked slightly for the next section (4.3).

PHOTOCALL 5 SEPTEMBER 2020

What:

Where:

Date:

Time:

Then add in a note about what facilities are available; e.g.,

Photo, video and interview opportunities available.

Wi-Fi access available.

Metered street parking available.

About PARAGRAPH

Write *one* succinct paragraph that explains what the event is about.

PHOTO, VIDEO AND RECORDING OPPORTUNITIES:

- What makes the picture noteworthy that the photographer can capture?

- Are there any experts, charity representatives, voice of authority, etc., that can be offered for interview?
- Any other succinct points that could be added?

ENDS
For further details, contact NAME, EMAIL and CONTACT number:

Editors' Notes:
Insert press release or additional information about story here.

When to issue a photocall

I often do a three-prong attack so issue a few weeks in advance to make sure it is in the diary and sent in advance. I then usually follow up a week in advance and I might even consider calling the day before to remind them/see if anyone is coming.

Exclusive option

If your picture/video is very strong, you may want to consider offering one of the newswires such as Reuters or the Press Association an exclusive. By offering exclusive access to an event you might be taking a risk, but if they do decide to go through with it and the picture takes off this can go viral.

TIPS

The dos

- The key principle of the picture is to make sure there is a who, what, why, when and where – make sure your picture can answer three of these.
- Do make sure that your picture tells the story, you should be able to tell what the story is without much explaining.
- Have a human interest where relevant; e.g., the artist making final touches to the wax work at Madame Tussauds, the customer taking a bite out of the quirky food dish.
- Make sure you take a range of story shots and don't just focus on one hero shot as you may find on the day that things change.
- Make sure you have a range (6–10) of landscape and portrait images that goes in your final edit.
- Embed a caption that tells the story of your image and include a credit to your photographer.
- Name your image.

The don'ts

- Just like a press release or press pitch, your picture needs to tell a story and not be an advertisement. So, don't heavily brand it because frankly they just won't use it.
- Take a picture for a timely occasion and then try and bank it for the following week. You need to

issue the picture the same day for news; e.g., you may very well have a bright sunny background and if you issue the following week when it is raining it is very obvious.
  — Don't issue too many images to picture editors or picture desks, too much choice is overwhelming and makes it more of a difficult task the other side.

CHECKLIST

  — Does your picture tell the story?
  — Have you created a caption of 8–10 words?
  — Have you embedded the caption?
  — Have you created a folder with hi-res images/ low-res images?
  — Are you checking online 'picture of the day' edits ahead of the day to get a feel for the sort of images that work?
  — Have you picked a day when there is not a huge amount of other activity happening that you might be competing against; e.g., Chelsea Flower Show, General Election, A-Level results day.

4.3 Video stories

Learning to make great video content should be an essential part of your marketing mix. Whichever media channel you use, video is the way forward and this is because Facebook, Instagram and LinkedIn want to become publishers. But you may also want to create a PR-able asset alongside your marketing content.

There are three ways I recommend small businesses work on video content:

1. Work with a video partner as part of a newswire; e.g., TNR – the picture arm of the Press Association.
2. Issue a videocall – similar to a photocall, except you are providing examples of video.
3. Issue your own video content – again following a similar pitching format to selling-in to picture desks but to video/digital desks.

For the purposes of the book, I'm going to focus on issuing a videocall as this requires zero budget other than your time.

ACTIVITY

- Using the photocall template from section 4.2, tweak for video and fill out for your campaign.
- Draft a press release or smaller media alert (a paragraph that explains the story).
- Cross-reference your target media identified from Chapter 1.4 and build out the database you created in Chapter 3.1. Consider building a separate video media tab for the titles you want to approach.
- Many video teams get booked far in advance such as *Cosmopolitan* or Business Insider, so consider giving as much as a month's notice for a quirky

pop-up or specific event so that they can get in the diary.
- Email your videocall, with your press release or media alert cut and paste underneath in one email.
- Follow up the week before or at latest 3/4 days before filming day to confirm attendance.

EXAMPLE

When Sutton & Sons announced they were launching a vegan-only branch, I did some research and realised that London did not in fact have a vegan-only branch. There was one in Bristol and one in Kent. So, we created the newshook of 'London's only fully vegan chip shop' and invited video teams to attend.

I issued out the videocall across:

- Newswires
- London TV and radio
- Food lifestyle sites
- A bunch of miscellaneous media that I thought might find it so random, they would cover it; e.g., LADbible, Buzzfeed's 'now Here this' and Business Insider.

For video assets we offered:

- Danny Sutton, owner of award-winning family-run business to talk about why his fish and chip shop was expanding into vegan

- Interviews with the chef on the recipe and cooking process of the banana blossom 'fish'
- Interviews with serving staff on popularity and a new crowd of customers coming through
- Case studies of vegans/non-vegans trying the vegan 'fish'
- Taste tests for presenters to try the vegan offering.

I pitched to each title differently with the broadcast notice; for example, for Bloomberg's video channel TicToc, I invited chief food critic Richard Vine, a notorious meat eater, to try the vegan food. Versus Reuters whom I offered interviews with the general public who were trying vegan for the first time for feedback on their thoughts about the food.

We offered early access for an exclusive for one of the newswires. Then went far and wide. On this occasion whilst we did pitch out the news release, we led with video and let this lead the rest of the coverage.

The video footage appeared on multiple stations across the UK on both TV stations, online for news outlets and we even appeared on eight international TV stations. The global reach of the campaign meant we were then approached by many vegan bloggers and publications, food reviewers and feature writers of the nationals directly, saving us half a job.

Retrospectively, after we had secured over 200 pieces globally, I had video teams approaching us to film for a fee, but obviously by this point we had already had video for free and huge global exposure.

TIPS

- Make sure your video is telling a story rather than trying to sell a product.
- Can you inject some irreverence, humour or something quirky?
- Is it worth holding the story as an exclusive or can you give one title exclusive access a few days in advance?
- Don't heavily brand your video because otherwise it will seem like branded content and you will be asked to be paid to place it.

CHECKLIST

- Have you provided all your contact details and the basics of who, what, where in your videocall notice?
- Have you provided plenty of assets for filming (remember you need to talk about "your viewers" rather than your readers)?

4.4 Influencer engagement

For businesses with little to no budget, working effectively with influencers can have a transformative effect on your business sales.

Influencer marketing is the term used for working with individuals with an engaged and higher following on social media platforms. When you work with the right influencer, you gain access to their friends, fans and audience who in theory should also be your target audience, and this endorsement automatically catapults your brand from an unknown entity into something positive and desirable.

There are a few ways you can work with influencers:

- *Building relationships directly* – where you contact the influencer yourselves. This works best if you are approaching smaller influencers and you are looking to gift the product in exchange for content – more of this in the Activity section below.
- *Working with a talent agency* – when you have a budget and want to pay the influencer to promote your product.
- *Working with a talent platform* – where you might have a larger pot that you can carve up and multiple influencers can submit their own content for your review in exchange for payment.

Mary Kate Trevaskis, co-founder, The Tape Agency talks to us about how you can work with a talent agency and emerging talent.

We contract exclusively with our talent in terms of brand social media partnerships. Our criteria for taking someone on is that, if the internet disappeared tomorrow, we would still have a reason to represent our talent, a reason to engage with brands and shout about their missions/projects and passions. We are basically the middle person in the conversation working to make everyone happy ultimately.

Influencers now have a unique selling power outside of media, and the key thing is to find the influencer that authentically sums up your brand message without sacrificing who they are or their tone of voice, otherwise the cut through to the followers and engagement won't be there and it is money wasted for the brand and time/reputation wasted for the talent.

ACTIVITY

The strategy and tactics you need to implement a successful influencer marketing campaign are not dissimilar to compiling a traditional media outreach so below I've summarised my top tips for getting started:

Research

Yes, I know you know that this is what I make you do, but do your homework. The first thing you need to do is come up with a list of experts, personalities or organisations you want to reach out to. Cross-reference this against your business objectives – are these people going to have an influence on your brand's target audience? Maybe even start with your own followers or Google local bloggers. Search hashtags related to your brand.

Ego check

I would strongly advise *not* going after the Top 10 influencers globally because a) they will want to be paid and b) it's unlikely that you can just build an authentic relationship and slide into their DMS. Think about people that might benefit from you, your product and service and maybe pick a range to see who and what is a driver for you. Test out both nano-influencers (fewer than 5,000 followers) and micro-influencers (5,000–100,000 followers). When you connect with someone with a niche following, chances are they have a very engaged audience *and* they will be grateful and honoured to work with you, so they are likely to be posting and sharing more with better engagement levels than someone with higher follower numbers.

Participation and appreciation

You want to be part of a culturally relevant dialogue that fits with your brand whether that is business or lifestyle. So, engage with everyone big and small who is leading and participating and see how they get engagement and how they add value and think about how you can do the same.

Is gifting the right thing? How else can you actually collaborate again? Try to think differently and try a few things. Maybe a guest takeover? A collaborative live video?

What success looks like to you

Much like traditional PR, are you looking to drive sales, awareness, new business leads? Track your numbers before you do a campaign and on a basic level, track immediate traffic and as many stats as possible like sales, engagement and followers after the campaign. If the campaign works well, who can you partner with to replicate the experience or what else can you do to enhance the relationship and take it further?

Don't pay over the odds

If someone comes back to you with an influencer/brand deck check them out. There are many free tools online to check engagement levels and costs per post. Check out influencermarketing.com who have an influencer money calculator to help you gauge what they are actually worth per post. There is a famous case of the girl who had millions of followers who couldn't even shift a minimum order number to sell t-shirts. So, make sure they are engaged.

Pick your niche wisely

It can be tempting to look at your competitors and try and go after their audience. But when you think about your brand – your unique selling point (USP) – can you dare to be different and go to a different space? A great example of this is MOJU: their drinks are a functional performance product, they don't play in the typical wellness space. Co-founder Rich Goldsmith says:

> There's brilliant products in the natural food space, but often brands struggle to make the leap to a mass market audience. Which is surely the aim if you want to make a big impact on the health of consumers. Brands are often dull or aimed at the "wellness" warriors, and feel exclusive and preachy. We felt there was a much bigger opportunity to reach a wider audience. An audience that aren't Gwyneth Paltrow fans or into yoga, but may be relying on heavily processed products as part of their active and busy lives.

Do nots

It should go without saying but just in case it doesn't, don't just spam a load of influencers. Take your time to build an authentic relationship with them. It's a two-way street, they should want to actually receive your product. I hear from a lot of small business owners who complain that they send out product and receive no response. This for me is a red flag that they have not taken the time to build a real relationship with this person in the first place.

EXAMPLE

Anyway, one of my good pals who runs Litwicks single-handedly grew her business using influencers on Instagram, so I asked her to give some anecdotes that other small business owners could learn from. To date, she has been stocked in Urban Outfitters, a range of boutiques across the UK and was invited to be an Amazon seller. Here is how Becky Cope, founder of Litwicks candles, did it.

> I set up my business on a shoestring, it was almost a test for me to see what I could make out of nothing. Instagram was my platform and I set out building my network of followers that in turn converted to customers. I knew my product was designed for females and could be personalised to suit the recipient so building relationships with influencers was key to broadening my reach.
>
> I made a list of people I followed and enjoyed watching on Instagram, likeminded females with a good following who, in return for a free candle, wouldn't mind posting a picture. I was so surprised by the reaction, instant sales, my first one generated £400 worth of revenue for the cost of one candle and the time spent forging a relationship, it was totally worth it.
>
> Results did vary and initially I was focused on influencers with c50k followers plus. However, my best results came from someone with 15k followers, her community was clearly very engaged, and it made me think about how Instagram stories are so much more powerful

than we think. In addition to gifts to posts, I also ran competitions with other similar brands, again I made a list and set out direct messaging them.

TIPS

—   Make sure you build a relationship with influencers first and remember they are real people with lives. Clemmie Telford @clemmie_telford offers this nugget:

Sometimes people send me things in the post speculatively and then hound me for a post. And its uncomfortable. Though on paper its lovely to receive gifts I'd prefer to be asked first and given the option to politely decline or to choose from their offering. e.g. if it's clothing, I might have a different idea of what suits my children or my home. People forget that its work: I curate two blog posts a week and post on Instagram every day, so assuming that a gift automatically equals an immediate piece of content is unrealistic. Perhaps I am testing the product, maybe I am waiting for the most relevant moment to share and occasionally the gift just isn't something I like.

—   Cultivate influence: James Lohan, Mr & Mrs Smith, tells us:

When we launched, a core part of our strategy was to work with culturally interesting and like-minded people. We trusted our own taste, but we felt the added clout of some more notable guests (Basement Jaxx's Felix Buxton, then *Sunday Times Style* editor Tiffanie Darke and star chef Raymond Blanc all featured in the first book) would reinforce it. Plus, we thought the hotel review itself was ripe for reinvention – less checking for dust on top of cupboards and more genuine tales of a real couple's trip. This was back before the term 'influencer' was even conceived but the principles are the same today. We wouldn't just partner with any old celebrity; it was about working with people who chimed with our founding principles: inspiring, stylish and thoughtful. By aligning the brand with these names it became an organic promotional tool. We still work with a roster of emerging and existing talent, only now on a much bigger scale, but sticking very closely to those core values.

CHECKLIST

- Are the influencers you're reaching out to people who you like or are they genuinely people that your audience likes?
- Is that influencer a natural consumer for your brand, product or service?

- Are you just following your competitors? Don't, if an influencer is connected to one brand, they can't then partner with another of the same type and equally, why would you want to?
- Have you built an authentic relationship with them? You don't want to effectively cold-call them with a DM.

4.5 Research

When trying to create a PR newshook, you are continually asking yourself who cares? Who cares? Who *cares*? And if you can't find something to talk about then creating a research angle can be a great way to get press interest.

I personally *love* a research story, but they are not for those who are risk averse. The reality is you often have one bite of the cherry to get your research covered by national news and if you pitch in on a busy news day you won't get a look in (like the time I phoned the Press Association to see if they were interested in my news story and at just that minute it had been announced Osama bin Laden had been captured – story over).

ACTIVITY

There are two options for research stories:

- Option 1: Create your own research
- Option 2: Work with a research partner.

I have had a story go viral using Option 1 (check the Hari Ghotra news example from Chapter 3.10), but it still required the client investing money to gather the data. I've worked with other tech and data companies who can use their own software to tell a qualitative story; e.g., AI transcription service Trint created a UK politicians' Trint Index to show who was the most easily understood by the robots (amazingly Maybot was the most understood by the tech).

That said, if you are a smaller consumer or business outlet my recommendation is to work with a partner and my preferred one is Censuswide. They help you craft your story, advise on the format of questioning to ensure that you get the right answers back and unlike some other suppliers I've tried don't bombard you with sales calls.

Six reasons for using a research partner are:

1. When working with a research partner, they will help you pull out the sort of headlines and then questions that are interesting.
2. As part of the briefing, I always provide a list of headlines or angles that could be interesting for my clients. By starting with headlines everyone can think about what is newsworthy, what might have already been done or how we could take the story on.
3. Once you agree the headlines you are interested in, you can work backwards to then craft your questions.

4. Your questions then go into the field and after a period of time you get the raw data back.

5. From here you can use the answers to develop a press release or news angle, looking through national newspapers, you will often see research-led quirky news stories at the front end of the paper.

6. Using ONS population statistics you can create some very media-worthy headlines beyond the people you have polled as long as you have a good enough segmentation; e.g., the current mid-year UK population statistics are 66 million (66,040,200: if 20% of your correspondents believe something, then you can take 20% of the ONS population statistics to say "13 million people think", etc.)

EXAMPLE

I spoke with Nicky Marks, managing director of Censuswide who provided the following introduction for those who don't know anything about getting a research story on the different approaches you can take:

1. Media specific
   There is a variety of ways that brands can use research to achieve press coverage and the type of survey you opt for would depend on what your target media is. The broadsheets will be looking for a slightly different style to the tabloids for example. We would always

advise that you work backwards in your decision-making process, so [you] have a firm idea of where you want the coverage to appear and then craft the story angle and question development around that.

2. Survey selection

There are a number of popular formulas for creative survey stories. One of which is pinpointing specific numbers or dates – for example, you may want to use your research to find out the cost of the average family meal or the cost of the average family holiday, or the date that most families will book their summer holiday for example – being as specific as you can with these figures will all help spark interest from the media. Other popular formulas include countdowns, 'top 10' or 'top 50' and 'what Brits don't know' highlighting areas where Brits are lacking in knowledge – for example, can they pinpoint where Sheffield is on a map? This formula also works really well for kids – do they know where honey or beef burgers come from?

3. Newsjacking

Another way of using research for press coverage is to be reactive to the current news. Using a fast 24-hour service on your surveys will allow you to react to the news agenda and brands can act as a voice, stating the public's point of view. If it has been a big news story, there will be a huge press appetite for follow ups, so this is a very effective method.

4. Brand support

Research is used in a variety of different ways for promotion, the most popular way is to support press coverage – but stats which highlight the views of the British public are beneficial in a variety of ways for brands. Stats are a great way of creating content for website[s] and blogs. It's very easy for brands to make claims on what they believe to be true but backing these up with real facts and figures give[s] these views gravitas and can help brands to position themselves as thought leaders in their spectrum. Stats are also commonly used for white papers which are published in the public domain.

5. A note on costs

When a research campaign is executed well, it can be a very cost-effective method. Whilst we would usually recommend running between 10–15 questions for a survey to maximise exposure, we have seen a number of successful campaigns run on as little as 2 questions. These campaigns can create huge traction, especially if a link goes viral and can create news content all over the world, which is also fantastic for SEO campaigns. Compared to standard advertising costs, it is a very affordable way of achieving exposure.

TIPS

- If you are doing a poll you need at least 1,000 respondents to have credibility.
- Ideally, you want to have 2,000 respondents nationwide to get a national news story.
- If you want to pitch a story to broadcast, I have often heard that they need a minimum of 3,000 correspondents.

CHECKLIST

- If you don't end up securing press coverage because of the news agenda that day, can you still use the research as a brand building tool? For example, can you create some thought leadership, guest posts, social media posts and a newsletter?
- Have you created the right research story for the publications that you want to be in?
- Has the story already been done and if so, how can you evolve it?
- Make sure the results are surprising if you want press coverage; an obvious trend or stat is not going to make the news.

4.6 TV

Due to the nature of the TV format there are multiple ways that everyday people can secure exposure on broadcast channels and you don't need to be a famous CEO of a global entity to have your business featured. In this section, I want to get you thinking about how you might be able to get on television with a few examples of slots that can work for small businesses/entrepreneurs.

ACTIVITY

So, if you want to get on TV then firstly, let's just go back to the drum beat. Does it hit your business objectives from Chapter 1.1?

- That's right. Do your homework! Research different shows. Just like you study a magazine or newspaper for slots that are relevant. Make sure you know exactly which segment it would be suitable for you to be featured in. And on a very basic level, know the name of who presents that segment and apparently, because it does need to be repeated a lot, spell it right.
- Once you know which slot works for you watch it a few times and really get a feel for the style of the segment and content.
- Can you add to your own story; e.g., if you are pitching a new product as part of a trend can you suggest some other brands that it can work with? Do you have any interesting spokespeople you can add to your story to give it more weight; e.g., an expert?
- Create your media list of producers for the shows that you want to be on, this isn't about having the longest list, it's about having a tight list of the most relevant.

- Try to send an email as early in the day as possible. I would always try before 10:00 am.
- Just to reiterate because it is crucial – your pitch to TV must be visual.
- Draft your expert pitch crib email. If a story breaks, you then only need to amend two bullet points in reaction, and you are ready to go.

EXAMPLE

Product placement slots

There are many day-time and weekend magazine style shows such as *This Morning*, *Good Morning Britain* and *Sunday Brunch*. Just like a cross between a newspaper and magazine they have a hybrid of slots. There is usually a topical news story/guest on the sofa, perhaps a magazine-style feature which might look at top tips for holiday packing, for example.

Marshmallowist CBD
As part of our strategy to secure coverage for The Marshmallowist CBD mallows, the pitch email was focused more on the growing trend of CBD products in the wellness space and we highlighted a few other products in the space to show the trend.

As part of on an ongoing sell-in to media, this story was then picked up by the *Daily Mail* who ran a full feature on CBD wellness trends and within a day we were contacted directly by the demo producer of *This Morning*. It is worth flagging that we had directly pitched to her twice before in the previous six months, but clearly the feature in national print had helped convince ITV that this was a major news trend. Online sales within the first 24 hours were up by 300% from the previous six months.

Regional newsjacking

If you are working on a local news story you should consider going to both your local BBC and ITV local news channels. A quick search on either website will give you the contact for your local news teams.

This could be a charity event, a quirky story or even as simple as owning a quirky location that could make good backdrop material for a broadcast. For a daily regional news programme, you might want to pitch a few days in advance or on the actual day.

Ask the expert

The most success I've had across my PR career is going down the 'expert' route. Thanks to the changing media landscape we have news breaking 24 hours a day and that means experts to comment on news stories are in constant demand. I would recommend creating an expert crib sheet that is tailored for broadcast.

Here is my sample expert for broadcast pitch:

> Title: Expert Happiness Consultant – Samantha Clarke
>
> Samantha Clarke is an expert who is able to talk confidently in response to breaking news story of 'Insert occasion here'.
>
> Pitch: Prepare 3–4 bullet points of things she can talk about; e.g.,
>
> - How focusing on workplace happiness can boost your business success.
> - Why employees need to take responsibility for their own work happiness.

Reactive space: perhaps it is World Happiness Day *or* a report has just been issued to say that Londoners are the most miserable workers in the country. The first bullet points in your pitch need to address the current breaking news, so your guest expert template will change with every pitch.

Sign off your email and underneath include a short bio to demonstrate experience, links to video (any) to show she is confident in front of a screen, contact email and phone number.

Include a small low-res photo – (just to show you don't look like a weirdo and don't have a face for radio).

Drafting an email like this costs nothing but your time, but pitched at a timely moment can be the equivalent of thousands.

Real-life case studies

I often talk about the two sides to client stories; e.g., the business story and the entrepreneurial story. If you would like help selling your own personal story to media, then you could consider approaching a service that sells-in stories themselves to TV and radio and is always on the hunt for interesting stories and often paying guests to be featured.

TIPS

- Keep it timely, a lot of shows are turned around exceedingly quickly so you don't want to waste your time by going too far in advance or too late in the day.
- If you can't find who to speak to try calling the switchboard and asking for the right contact email.
- Talk your pitch out loud, what is the real story and can you sell it in with just a few sentences?
- What assets do you have that work for TV, think about who you are offering as a speaker and what they can talk about, can you offer a unique location or background that will make filming easy? Remember TV is visual so you want to be

providing ideas for why you/your story could work visually.

- Don't be egocentric, regional TV news has highly engaged audiences.
- You don't want to be pitching why your business is so great, producers don't care about promoting you. They care how it relates to their audience. So, what is the 'viewer benefit' of you being on TV?

A note before you appear on TV:

- We are all nervous speakers but a bit of media training or practising of what you want to say can work wonders.
- Comedians are notorious for fitting lots of information into their shows and often have a few words as prompts. Think about what the key points are that you want to land and have as prompts.
- Don't script yourself, by all means rehearse but you don't want to sound like a robot.
- Don't wear anything too jazzy or too small/tight or a print.
- Make sure you arrange recording of the show you will appear on so you can share.

A note after you appear on TV:

- Thank the producer/booker for booking you – if you forge a relationship there is a good chance you will be booked again.

- Cut and share the video clip of you afterwards, add it to your expert crib sheet to demonstrate your ability on air. If you have a press section on your website, put it here, include links on your other social channels.
- Put it on your LinkedIn and remind your followers from time to time you did TV by resharing. You don't need to just use it once.

CHECKLIST

- Make sure you have totally nailed your business one-liner as created in Chapter 2.1.
- Ensure your key talking points and awareness days are relevant for your business and match. Have them prepared ready for a timely broadcast pitch. You need to make sure that what you pitch is relevant to what is happening at this very moment.
- Identify national trends that you can speak about as an expert and have an actual point of view. How is your perspective unique?
- Consider some public speaking or media training to perfect your presentation skills.
- Always give a phone number, TV does not work 9–5 and they may need to contact you at a moment's notice.

4.7 Radio

It surprises many people to know that radio is one of the top media that Brits not only listen to on a regular basis, but it is one of the most trusted sources. Hence me giving radio its own section as it is an often-overlooked channel. Who wouldn't want to be on one of the topical shows on Radio 4, for example, whose listening figures continue to increase with a reach of over 2.871m?[2]

To give us a bit of insight into the different types of radio, we spoke with Aaron from Abeat Media who broke down the key programmes and listenership:

Nationals such as Sky News, Radio 2 and 5Live (UK Wide coverage 1–5 million listeners)

Major regionals (over 250,000 listeners) such as BBC Radio Kent, BBC Radio Leeds, BBC Radio Newcastle, BBC Radio Merseyside, BBC Manchester and BBC London.

Commercial radio (between 125,000 [and] 249,999 listeners)… includes Moray Firth Radio, Hallam FM, Metro Radio and Free Radio.

Key regional radio (between 50,000 & 124,999 listeners) such [as] BBC Somerset, BBC Radio Oxford, BBC Northampton, BBC Gloucestershire, BBC Radio York and commercials such as Star Radio, Swansea Sound and Juice Brighton.

---

[2] RAJAR (Radio Joint Audience Research) Q2 2017.

Typical regional radio (20,000 to 49,999 listeners) such as BBC Jersey and BBC Guernsey.

ACTIVITY

- Go back to your list of media created in Chapter 1.4 and if you have not already done so think about the radio stations your audience would engage with.
- Listen to the actual shows, get a feel for the different presenting styles and chat segments.
- Instead of your tear sheets, write down the programmes/slots that would be relevant for your business and add to the media database you created in Chapter 3.1.
- Review all the guest post and feature ideas you created in Chapter 2.5 and 2.6 and think about how these could be applied for radio.
- Are there any relevant calendar dates or national days that you are specifically qualified to speak about from Chapter 1.6?
- Listen to the shows on a regular basis.
- Look for the contact details for the producer of that show. These can usually be found with an intuitive search on the website.
- You need to ensure you are contacting the planner, researcher or producer of that show and *not* the presenters.

EXAMPLE

Real-life case study: Money Medics is a business that aims to empower millennials to talk about money. They use first-person real-life examples of their own business to gain traction. So rather than pitching to *Money Box* on Radio 4 with "Hey we are an expert in personal finance and have a business that aims to empower millennials", they can say "Hey, I've got a story on how I saved £10k in my first year after university and bought my first house before 25".

TIPS

Johnny Seifert is the showbiz editor for talkRADIO as well as producer for the *Badass Women's Hour XL* and hosts his own podcast *Secure The Insecure* where he talks to reality stars about their insecurities. Here he gives his eight Top Tips for how to pitch to radio:

1. I will contact newspaper journalists if I like a story that I have seen written that is a life story but welcome speculative pitches from interesting stories who have made it into the paper who might then contact to say [here is] a link to a story I appeared in today – and I'm available should you wish to cover X, Y & Z further.

2. If you are struggling to find contact details for the show, check media.info for individual contact details or Twitter. Most producers will have their email in their Twitter bio. Twitter is also good for people to be responsive to requests or build relationships with producers.

3. I'm sure I'm not alone in receiving 100s of emails so keep your pitch succinct, three lines ideally – Dear (insert person's name and *spell* it correctly). If you spell my name wrong, you don't even get a look in. Be really clear on what you do and what the story is and a clear reason of why you want to be on, focused on how it will be of interest to our listeners rather than benefit yourself (and make sure you spell the station name correctly).

4. I personally like and use press releases, even if you are pitching a story about you having depression for example, the press release is what I use as background material for the presenters and brief them on questions.

5. I would recommend not asking for interview questions because if you rehearse your answers it can lack the emotion when it is a live recording. If you are interested in speaking radio then there is a good chance you are already an expert in what you speak on so you won't need to read from a piece of paper.

6. Make sure you can own what you say, debates work really well, and we welcome strong opinions, but you can't take it back afterwards. And remember, if a debate we feature goes viral then it can mean free advertising for your business. Just make sure it is working for you and your brand.

7. If you want to pitch off a national newshook e.g. World Kindness Day and you are an expert with something punchy to say about this then I would email one week before and again on the day (before 8am) – that is the sort of thing that can easily go on the Drive Time show for example.

CHECKLIST

– Seek some media or public speaking training if you are keen to get more experience.

– Know the show inside out, what time is it on, what are the different segments called? Demonstrate in your pitch that this is an email that is written for them.

– Make sure you have availability, the last thing you want to do is pitch yourself, get booked and then let them down, this is not the way to get good media relations, my friend.

– Don't forget about your BBC local news stations, particularly for a light-hearted local news story.

– Make sure your spokesperson has not been featured heavily in the last six months.

4.8 Social media for PR

A word of caution: I 100% advocate small business owners using social media to Hype Yourself, *but* this should not be the only part of your promotion strategy. I use social media to support my wider promotional campaigns, and in this section, I'm going to give you examples of the best way to use social channels for the purpose of hyping your business.

Twitter

Meet the media

Above and beyond any other social media platform, Twitter is the best free resource to connect with media and understand what they are looking for.

Search the hashtag, #journorequest, select 'latest', and you will see a steady stream of journalists looking for spokespeople, case studies or businesses for interview.

In the past day as of this writing, I have pitched for a national newspaper and a major radio show and found two journalists who are relevant to a specific story I'm working on.

Twitter lists

People (me) can often get inundated by the sheer amount of information going on in Twitter. I've found using Twitter lists an essential part of keeping track of a few tailored groups that are bespoke to me and my business.

So, what the dang are Twitter lists? Think of it like a WhatsApp chat group with your best pals. The difference being that maybe you don't know these people and maybe they are on an aspirational list.

I have a few lists:

- *Cool venues*: I always like to follow new spaces that are opening up and get a feel for the sort of events they are showcasing. It's like brand food.
- *Start-up journalists*: These are the journalists that, whatever the client, I need to know inside out. The articles they share give me an idea of what is currently topical. And I can see when they are looking for ideas and contributors.
- *Innovative businesses*: I believe that learning in business is never done. To be an expert you need to constantly be evolving and learning and therefore keeping an eye on what other brilliant businesses are doing helps to keep me and the businesses I work with on their toes.
- *New journalists*: Often if I help out a journalist or meet them at an event I want to try and keep that relationship warm where possible. So, I have a private list of new contacts I've made or discovered and want to build a relationship with to remind me these are the people I need to build engagement with.

Comment, engage and share
Twitter is in my humble opinion the best platform for breaking news and trends. I have a few hashtag searches I do on the regs or use my list of relevant journalists to look at the articles being shared and will RT, comment or share on breaking stories as well as sharing 'best in practice' PR stories. It is also perfect to share your own blog posts, award wins or press coverage and with a raft of programming tools you can do this in advance. I know, for example, my blog post on how to write a business bio always performs really well so it's worth me rescheduling this to go out. Also, by sharing on different days and times you can get a feel for when is the best time to engage with your audience.

Contact details
Make it really easy for prospects to contact you and include these in your Twitter bio. Also write your area of expertise in your bio. Often producers/researchers looking for a particular expert will use Twitter to find them. Equally you can find many journalists' contact details via Twitter.

Instagram

A visual business snapshot
Journalists use Instagram to get a quick snapshot of what a business is about. They don't look at likes and followers,

but they do look at what you are saying. For your own business consider a blend of:

- Sharing the best of your client work
- Demonstrate your own achievements and small wins
- Provide tips and expertise that showcase your knowledge
- Best in practice: share content of the best in your area
- Show your face in one in every nine pictures to remind people of the person behind the business
- Selling – be cautious of only using Instagram grid as a selling platform but if you are selling, make sure your page is shoppable
- You can use up to 30 hashtags on the grid and 10 on your stories to be easily searchable.

Make it look visually pleasing
Try not to re-use the same photography. It is totally fine to use other photography in the public space if you are crediting the original source and tagging them. Collages look like clip art from the early 90s word processor programmes, so avoid. Try to incorporate your brand look and personality throughout so maybe use a colour palette and stick to your brand guidelines. For colour palette help, look at www.instagram.com/colours.cafe or for images – try Unsplash, Shutterstock or Getty Images.

Share all the links

It's almost pointless putting a link in your insta caption because nobody can click on it, as we are all looking at insta on our phone it's a bit too fiddly to cut and paste. Consider using a service like Linktree. You can have multiple links and the paid-for platform is very affordable and you can see which links are performing well and change accordingly.

Encourage UGC

How can you encourage more user generated content? If you are selling books, for example, can you share strong imagery from your audience of your book out in the wild rather than the same front cover cut up in different ways? That way you can tag the person who shared the book and convert them into a follower of your product/ service if they were not already. You could even reward shared content with a prize.

Facebook

FB Business Groups

Networking groups – without doubt the most helpful *free* resources and advice I have gleaned for myself and for a lot of my clients, is being part of networking groups where people knowledge share. From accountancy tips, to growth pains, to assessing whether one online course is right for you or not. LIGHTBULB is a great group created by Charlotte Fall.

Local/regional groups
An underused resource is local FB groups. Many have special days where they allow business owners to plug any special deals, events, etc. It's also a great way to connect and cross-collaborate with other businesses in your local area to grow your platform.

FB Stories
Getting traction on your FB newsfeed is very difficult, but as mentioned previously with every social media channel looking to grow into publishers, video content will take precedence so try to share as much on stories as possible.

LinkedIn

As mentioned previously, if you could put all your chips on one platform, then LinkedIn is my platform of choice at the moment and I'm amazed at how many small businesses aren't utilising this platform enough.

Sharing guest articles
If you want to prove your credentials as an expert, then writing an article for LinkedIn on a regular basis is a really easy win to raise your profile. You can also then use these as examples of your writing when pitching to media.

Video is the best way to engagement
Think of it this way, when you speak on a panel event you might hit 100–200 people. But sharing a video on

LinkedIn can easily amass 5,000 views almost overnight. So, lose your cringe, pull on your big pants and start sharing your face on camera.

You don't have to connect with people
You can now follow connections such as journalists or marketing partners to keep abreast of their content and build your relationships with them.

LinkedIn can be a great free focus tool
When I was looking for feedback on my book cover, my network and then their network all provided really useful feedback. Asking genuine questions will drive engagement with your profile as well as provide useful feedback.

Connect immediately
After an event or meeting, immediately connect with your new relationships on LinkedIn, you might not mutually serve each other now but as your careers progress there may very well be crossover where you can collaborate.

4.9 Business book

The possibilities of using a business book to Hype Yourself have become evident to me as I'm writing this book. Part of my mission is to support as many small businesses as possible with their publicity and writing a book fully supports the objectives that I outline in Chapter 1.

Writing a book is unlikely to make you millions but if you want to:

- Raise your industry profile
- Secure paid-for speaking opportunities
- Become a teacher/lecturer in your industry
- Have ambitions to sell coaching, courses or workshops

then writing a business book is going to assist.

ACTIVITY

There are two ways to get your business book out there, you can either self-publish or you can seek a business publisher. Whichever option you take, you do need to write a business book proposal.

I secured my publishing deal with Practical Inspiration Publishing after taking part in Alison Jones's Extraordinary Business Book Challenge which was a 10-day course. At the end of this, you will have completed a proposal template that you can either use to send to publishers or you at least have a framework to write your own book.

If you have a framework for the different elements of your book, then as you are writing blog posts and guest content as part of your content marketing strategy, use the chapter topics and segments of your book to craft them. This way you can actually draft the content for your book as part of your current job.

EXAMPLE

I feel like I'm in a cosmic Catch 22 writing a book about how to PR yourself, talking about how to write a book about how to PR yourself... *But* here are a few of the opportunities I have had already since announcing I'm writing a book.

- Invited to speak on multiple podcasts as a PR expert and the book deal is always something I am asked about.
- From struggling to pitch hosting my own events, I am now being paid to host panels and workshops.
- Generated email sign-ups with people registering for further information about the book to whom I can also look to upsell my future online courses and 2020 strategy.
- I've already secured multiple guest post slots for the six months in the run-up to the book being published as well as event invitations for book signings and speaking post-launch to continue to drive momentum.

TIPS

From attending the business book proposal challenge, there were two very clear camps. Those who wanted to write a business book but didn't have a firm idea of what they were writing vs those who were *very* clear in what they were doing.

- So, my first tip would be, spend time thinking about your book, read other business books from your area and think about what you do like and don't like.
- Think about how your book can be used as a promotional tool to deliver for your business.
- Make sure the book is fully aligned with what you want to do as a business. I want to be seen as a PR expert for small businesses. My book helps me do exactly that.

CHECKLIST

- Is your book clear and concise with brand clarity and working with your business goals?
- Will your book help you become a thought leader?
- Can you segment the writing of your book into multiple blog posts you can place as guest content?
- Have you created a marketing strategy that starts six months from before the book launches to the six months afterwards?

Chapter summary

Learning how to Hype Yourself is a bit like writing a book, you have your introduction, where you plan and prep; the main chunk/storyline – which is where you are pitching out and doing the execution of plan to get your story out there; and finally – just as we are at the conclusion now, the work doesn't end here. Here is my final checklist for making sure you are regularly Hyping Yourself. Consider checking this off monthly:

Strategy in action

Review your PR plan on a monthly basis
- What has worked well?
- What hasn't worked and what can you do to rectify this?
- What single thing can you do today that will benefit your long-term communications plan?
- What is happening in six weeks, three months, six months that you need to action?

Media toolkit in action

Check over your media toolkit
- Is your biography up to date across all social channels?
- Do you need new press photography or a little refresh? Does your photography still fit you?
- Do you need to revise your pitches for guest posts? What do you want to be talking about in the next few months?

Press Office

What have you achieved in your press office this month?
- Have you secured enough guest panels, posts, competitions, partnerships?

- Have you attended enough events?
- Have you written your newsletter/blog posts?
- What successes have you had? Have you shared them across your own marketing channels?
- Have you kept all networking contacts warm?

Outside the box

What can be done differently?
- Are you reading magazines, listening to podcasts, attending talks to be inspired?
- Have you tried something new to get yourself out there? Even if it is as small as a DM to a new contact, sharing a live video, creating a quiz, hosting a breakfast event?

ANY OTHER BUSINESS

The dreaded agenda point that can go on for hours in an inter-agency meeting, *but* I felt it was worth having a section of areas that didn't make it into the book proper that I still think are worth you considering.

Other considerations

Branding and design

Good branding isn't just about having a logo. It is the way you express yourself without saying a word. Whether I share a post on LinkedIn, give a presentation or if you come into my office, The Wern signature style and brand colours always come through and are instantly recognisable. A lot of small businesses struggle to see the return on investment for paying for good design, but if I tell you that after my brand refresh my organic new business enquiries grew by 400% then I hope this makes you think twice. After PR my biggest self-investment is branding and design and without it, I would not have the confidence in what I am hyping or the success. We live in a visual world so make sure you are making the biggest impact visually. Pictures can say an awful lot more than words.

Website

Quite simply – you need one. And at the very least, just have a holding page which has your contact details and a place to register your email. Many small businesses think that if they are not selling online or don't have the money, they should not have a website, but it is a key part of your promotional toolkit. If people Google you and can't find you, then all your promotional efforts are done in vain.

Sponsored posts/advertising

I have only dipped my toe in the sponsored post pool but that doesn't mean to say you shouldn't invest in this area. I see a lot of small businesses doing really well by working with specialist consultants in this area. Where possible, I've tried to keep the hyping ideas free and specifically from the PR umbrella.

Newsletters

I am probably asked a question about how to use Instagram as a PR tool every day but am never asked about newsletters. Going back to your business objectives, I am almost certain that writing a newsletter will serve you with these so if you convert the hours you spend from insta onto crafting a newsletter you could probably create something that is really kick-ass. The exposure of a newsletter is easily 10 times whatever you post organically on social and crucially these are your contacts — it doesn't change from an algorithm. If you were going to pick one element from the marketing mix to invest in — I would go all in for a newsletter every day of the week.

Partnerships

I mention this in the influencer section but speaking to some great startup brands out there it has become apparent that in the early days, marketing partnerships can be a fantastically lucrative way to hype your brand. Grace Gould, co-founder of Soda Says comments: "We really focus on partnering with likeminded brands. In the US we've done a great job partnering with smaller brands who target a similar audience than us, co-hosting dinners, events, cross email list giveaways."

Networking

All of the work you have done in Chapters One and Two should help you prepare yourself for networking. I could have easily written a whole segment dedicated to how to Hype Yourself at networking as even the introvert in me can find it hard work sometimes. How you chat to others at an event and how you follow up with them is all part of the hype machine. My top three takeaways for you are:

1. Know your one-liner and what you are about to be able to tell people about your business.

2. Connect with other attendees or panellists on social media ahead of the event. Then when you speak with them on the day you are not going in cold.

3. Follow up with everyone you meet within 24 hours with something actionable to not lose the momentum of the relationship you have just built.

Are you really ready?

I've often been approached by people who want my support with PR when they still have not fully defined their offering *or* made their website watertight. The problem with these things is you always want to be going out to media at the top of your game with the correct message. Changing your proposition or not being fully ready to promote it is just confusing. Equally, going viral can cause websites to crash and businesses to collapse. So, make sure you do have the infrastructure in place.

Let the business speak for itself

It might be that actually focusing on Hyping Yourself is something you need to do further down the line whilst you are building your proposition. I've included a small business case study here from US-based Vinyl Me, Please.

Co-founder Matt Fiedler comments:

> We funded the launch of Vinyl Me, Please by maxing out our personal credit cards. We didn't

have much of a marketing budget, much less a PR, so we had to get creative when thinking about growth. We decided to invest all of our time (which at that point was "free") into making the product and overall experience as noteworthy as possible. We knew if we could impress a small group of people, those people would tell their friends, and if we could impress those people, they would tell their friends. That worked, and eventually, the people we started to reach were well beyond our personal networks, many of whom happened to be writers. They recognized what we were doing as novel and unique and thought it was something their readers would be interested in knowing about. We got a lot of coverage in small to mid-level publications, which led to more and more coverage, and eventually coverage in major publications (we didn't pay for any of it). It turned into a groundswell of awareness that ultimately allowed us to quit our jobs and pursue VMP full time.

Keep on hyping

Once you have secured press coverage, a guest slot on a speaker panel, a podcast invite, etc., it doesn't end there. Make sure you document all of your appearances on a spreadsheet. Are you sharing all of your opportunities?

CHECKLIST

- Share all articles/podcasts/panel events across the social media channels you use (for event appearances, even flag several times pre-event).
- Document content live from an event appearance or when you are discovering interesting or useful content online.
- Share your success across all your social channels.
- Can you cut up and share the content you are in and schedule with quotes/links across your social channels?
- Include the mastheads of any publications you appear in on your website for your 'As seen on XX' section.
- Can you see an uplift in web traffic using Google Analytics on the days the coverage appeared?

The journey of Hyping Yourself isn't just about getting there – share your learnings. Share how you secured great opportunities, people are always intrigued and thrilled to know how it works.

If you can't meet an opportunity, put one of your own contacts forward, everything is about building and boosting your relationships and you may in turn receive some great opportunities.

Your press coverage doesn't die, you don't need to only share it once, find new ways of dissecting and sharing with your audience.

WHEN TO HIRE A PR AGENCY OR BOOK SOME PR COACHING

Many PR freelancers offer very affordable coaching packages and specialise in entrepreneurs and startups, so even if you can't afford the full cost of a bigger agency on retainer full-time you may be able to find specialist support to assist you in the following areas:

Crisis communications

Whether you hire a consultant to help you with the preparation of a pre-emptive crisis Q&A document (because in the heat of a crisis the last thing you want to be doing is scrambling around to find someone who can help you with your crisis comms) or you have a breaking story that you need support with in responding to, a PR pro will be able to help you with your response.

Launch support

Perhaps you already have an internal team that can do a launch but you need some help and guidance on carrying it out. Or perhaps you have had some investment and you want to create a bigger splash.

Press release not landing?

If you have been issuing a press release and all you have heard back is crickets, then a PR can be well placed to help look at other angles or amplify your existing press assets to sell-in to media.

Guest posts, panels and podcasts

Don't have the time to pitch yourself? Then you could consider collaborating with some PR resource to do this for you.

Reactive press

What a larger agency does well is help provide ideas and execute a reactive press office. This is because they will have a whole team scouring the news throughout the day who can flag industry topics that you need to react to.

DON'T BELIEVE THE HYPE?

If you have made it this far, I would like to thank you for taking the time to learn the craft of self-hype with me. I hope that this book has shown you the value of PR and how for nothing else but the cost of your time, you too could make significant growth in your business.

If you are still in any doubt, I hope that showing you how I have created my own lifestyle business with a six-figure turnover using the art of hyping alone demonstrates that it is an effective mechanism. I have never been in a competitive pitch, I regularly turn away clients and projects that don't fit my own business agenda and I'm continually learning and evolving my craft.

If I could give one piece of advice, it is that good PR is more than just about telling your story once – it is the narrative thread that should underpin all your business activity and to keep consistent with this you must treat yourself like your most important client.

Even sat in my garden office at home, I am still hyping myself through the expertise I share on social channels, the connections I am following up with, the guest posts I am writing, the newspapers and magazines I regularly read. Knowing who you are, what your business is about and why you do it is essential groundwork for building a strong communications programme.

Please follow me on whatever your preferred social channel is – on @wernchat to hear my latest hints, tips and tricks to Hype Yourself or sign up for our newsletter. If you have any questions, success stories or tips to share with me, please also use #hypeyourself. It would be lovely to see a movement of all the amazing small businesses out there championing each other to grow.

Keep on hyping.

Lucy x

(aka Wern)

USEFUL RESOURCES

Suppliers & Websites

ABC – Audit Bureaux of Circulations – Media circulations

Censuswide – Affordable research agency

CoverageBook – A tool for presenting and analysing reach of your press coverage

Gorkana – A journalist database tool, can be very expensive if you are a small company

media.info – Find the contact details of all commercial radio stations

Press Association – One of the UK's longest established newswires

PressPlugs – A paid-for service that provides inbound journalist requests

ResponseSource – A paid-for service that provides inbound journalist requests

Reuters – More business-led, but increasingly moving more into lifestyle

SWNS – A newswire that also looks for real-life stories to sell into media

TNR – The video desk of the Press Association

KEY TERMS

Boiler plate – A body of copy that doesn't change that sits at the bottom of your press release

B2B – A business that serves other businesses; e.g., The Wern

B2C – A business that serves consumers; e.g., The Marshmallowist

Embargo – If you issue a press release 'Under Embargo' it means the reporter you have sent it to can't publish a word until the date and time of the embargo

Feature – A trend-led article

Influencer marketing – A form of marketing using social media influencers to promote your content

#journorequest – Search for this term on Twitter to find journalists looking for stories

Long lead – A 3–6-month advance notice to pitch to a publication, applicable for monthly magazines like *Vogue*, *GQ* and *Condé Nast Traveller*

Media outlet – Could be newspaper, magazine, radio or TV (wherever your story is put out into the world)

Media relations – dealing directly with journalists

Mid lead – Usually 6–8 weeks advance notice needed for a weekly magazine to be told about news

Press release – The one-page crib sheet that explains your business

Sell-in – The process of 'selling' your story to the press

Short lead – A title that works with a very short lead time

RECOMMENDED READING

Big Magic – Elizabeth Gilbert

Be More Pirate – Sam Conniff Allende

The Tipping Point – Malcolm Gladwell

Do Open: How a Simple Email Newsletter Can Transform your Business – David Hieatt

Oversubscribed – Daniel Priestly

This Book Means Business – Alison Jones

ACKNOWLEDGEMENTS

Fiz Osborne, Ruth Ingram, Becky Cope, Joe Makertich, Davinia Tomlinson, Sophie Raine, Hadrien Chatelet, Victoria Dove, Jenny Simms, Oonagh Simms, Rich Goldsmith, Jimmy Cregan, Sarah Drumm, Samantha Clarke, Kate Mander, Jess Austin, Jules Pearson, Rebecca Denne, Kate Hollowood, Hana Sutton, Jo Tutchener-Sharp, Clemmie Telford, James Lohan, Grace Gould, Nicky Marks, Johnny Seifert, Jeremy Carson, Kathryn Wheeler, Sarah Orme, Loulla-Mae Eleftheriou-Smith, Matt Fiedler, Mary Kate Trevaskis and of course Alison Jones and the squad at Practical Inspiration Publishing.